Letters from a Little Black Cat

LETTERS
from a little black
CAT

Joy Herring

Letters from a Little Black Cat

Copyright © Joy Herring 2021

All rights reserved. This book may not be reproduced in whole or part, stored, posted on the internet, or transmitted in any form or by any means, electronic, mechanical, photocopying, recording, or other, without permission from the author of this book.

This publication is meant as a source of valuable information for the reader; however, it is not meant as a substitute for direct expert assistance. For direct advice, the services of a qualified professional should be sought. The author disclaims any responsibility for liability, loss or risk, personal or otherwise, that happens as a consequence of the use and application of any of the contents of this book.

This book reflects the author's present recollections of experiences over time. For various reasons some names, characteristics and identifying details have been changed, some events have been compressed, and some dialogue has been recreated.

Front cover image designed by Trish Hart

Typeset by BookPOD

ISBN: 978-0-6451746-0-1 (pbk) eISBN: 978-0-6451746-1-8

 A catalogue record for this book is available from the National Library of Australia

To Tim, Caroline and Fenella,
who came on this journey with me,
and to all lovers of cats around the world.

Contents

Tootsie and Tammy – My Childhood Pets	1
Meggie – My First Rescued Cat	7
Joffrey – the Kitten Who Wanted to Live	17
Bella – the Journey of an Angry Cat	35
A Day Out at the Nursing Home	61
Poppy	67
Pedigree Cats in Rescue	79
Cats in Welfare	93
Oliver's Army	105
Bonnie and Matilda	119
Albie – the Store Cat	143
Letters from a Little Black Cat	169
Acknowledgements	225
About the Author	228

Tootsie and Tammy – My Childhood Pets

Cats have always held a fascination for me right from childhood. My parents had sold their business in the small country town in Western Australia that I grew up in, and moved out to permanently live on the farm they had pioneered together.

It was especially exciting for me because I was the youngest child by a long stretch with my mother having had a little surprise arrive in her forties. My eldest brother had already left home to pursue his own farming life and my sister and other brother were away at boarding school in Perth.

My first close encounter with Tootsie the shed cat, as she was called, was when our house was being built. We lived in our shearing shed with bits of AAA class wool hanging from rafters where the wool classer had overthrown the fleece. The smell of lanolin from the oily floor permeated the air, counteracted by icy blasts from a southerly wind coming up through the race. Tootsie used to climb into bed with me and snuggle up for the night, both of us luxuriating in the warmth of each other. In the morning I would wake up with her gone. She was usually waiting patiently with my father, who after milking the cow would give her a bowl of fresh warm milk.

Being an undesexed farm cat, as most cats were, Tootsie had lots of kittens and I adored spending time with them. Tootsie was a pure white cat but quite often her babies were a mixture of colours with the occasional pure white ones in the mix.

After the school bus had dropped me off at the gate I would ride my bike quickly home, grab a bite to eat, then go down to the shed to spend time with Tootsie and her babies.

The kittens were gaining in strength, playing and starting to run around. They were so much fun and kept me entertained for hours before I was called to go home for dinner.

One day after arriving home from school, there were no kittens but Tootsie was there, patiently waiting for me to arrive.

'Where are your kittens?' I demanded to know.

Tootsie looked at me in a satisfied way as if to say, 'It's just you and me today. Time for lots of cuddles.'

I wasn't at all satisfied with a smooching cat and demanded she show me where her kittens were. Searching all over the shed and surrounds with Tootsie closely following, I once again demanded to know what she had done with her babies.

Tootsie seemed to sense my concern and started meowing before moving off in the direction of the paddock.

I started to follow her; after all, I had been watching *Lassie* on our newly bought black and white TV. Lassie was an intelligent dog who showed her master the way to save someone. Tootsie was my Lassie so I dutifully followed her through the gates and along some paddocks. Eventually we came to a heap of old logs pushed together ready to be burnt. From within the pile came the sound of tiny mewing, growing louder and more desperate as Tootsie placed herself among her kittens. Mumma had arrived and so had their milky feed time.

In my childish mind I was disgusted that Tootsie had brought her babies out to these dirty old logs so far from her comfortable bed in the shed. What sort of mother was she?

After their short feed I then placed the kittens into my jumper, carrying them all home to the safety of their bed in the shed. Tootsie followed quietly behind.

The next day after school I followed my normal routine of going down to the shed to play with the kittens. They weren't there but Tootsie was.

Once again, I played the Lassie trick and demanded to know where the kittens were. 'What have you done with them?' I asked in a stern tone. Tootsie looked at me, then started to lick her paws. She was not going to budge.

I again demanded she show me where she had taken the kittens. Tootsie kept licking her paws and finally groomed the rest of her soft white fur in total exasperation. This poor little cat had obviously spent all night carrying each kitten in her mouth, one by one, back to wherever she had chosen to teach them life skills. She was exhausted and no amount of coaxing by me was going to make her bring them back. I just had to accept the inevitable.

After what seemed like ages but in all probability was a week, she brought the kittens back to the shed. I was a lonely child so I was ecstatic that my playmates had come back.

Eventually my parents said the kittens had to go to new homes and leave the farm. Sometimes people did arrive to collect one of our kittens and I would sadly wave them goodbye. The other kittens would also disappear but it wasn't until years later I learnt that my father had put them in a sack with some stones and thrown them into a dam. That was the way things were controlled in those days. So many kittens, so disposable.

The compensation was that I was allowed to keep one of the kittens from a litter and she was another pure white cat we called Tammy.

It came time for me to go to boarding school in Perth and I was quite a miserable child there. I hadn't grown up with many children or siblings around so my friends were the farm animals and I missed them. Especially Tammy, my sweet little white cat, and Topsy, my Border Collie Kelpie cross dog.

For some reason Tammy was naturally sterile so the line of pure white farm cats ended with her passing. That didn't mean that there weren't other cats around though. Being so disposable, people used to drive along the road, see a dam, stop their car and throw the cat out. Their reasoning was that it would be alright because the cat had somewhere to drink from and there might possibly be other animals drinking there that it could eat. How people could think that way always disgusted me and still does. The cats would turn semi-feral in their fight for survival and the only measure to deal with them was to shoot them. I hated hearing the sound of the gun going off as some animal had to die.

The day before I came home on school holidays, the most extraordinary thing used to happen. Tammy used to come up to the house and wait by the back door. She knew she wasn't allowed into the house so just patiently waited outside. My mother used to go out and talk gently to her saying, 'She will be home tomorrow.' How did this little farm cat know I would be coming home? That was my first lesson on how special cats could be and what respect they deserved.

It wasn't the first time Tammy would come up to the house, because while I was on holidays, I used to sneak her in through the flywire window and onto my bed. What a wonderful greeting there was between us with her purring her heart out with all the affection I was placing on her and me being so happy back in my own bed on the farm with my adored cat.

Sneaking Tammy into my room did have consequences, though. While I was away at school, there was a night when my father went into the spare room next to mine to sleep, probably because his snoring was keeping my mother awake. Realising someone was in the room, Tammy sprang up to the windowsill and carefully pulled at the flywire until there was enough room for her to squeeze in.

My father must have been in a deep sleep when Tammy started to nuzzle him around the head. A quick swiping reaction from my father sent Tammy flying across the room but not before she had tried to cling to the closest thing within reach – my father's head. Being mostly bald, he was left with deep red welts across his forehead and head, which took a bit of explaining whenever he met anyone, and left most sniggering with laughter.

That was the end of my nightly reunions with Tammy. She was forbidden to come up to the house anymore and was scolded whenever she tried.

After Tammy passed away and the snow-white line of Tootsie ended, my parents adopted two fluffy ginger cats and surprisingly they were allowed to be house cats. They were the most affectionate, sweet-natured cats but the biggest surprise was my father's complete turnaround in how he viewed cats. They weren't working animals keeping the mice population low but pets that loved to sit on laps. The war had taken its toll on my father's health and he would often be found in a lounge chair stretched out with a ginger cat on his lap. I would never have believed it if I hadn't seen it with my own eyes – he was like a converted zealot in his affection for them. He adored them, and in return, they adored him.

Meggie – My First Rescued Cat

Like many Aussies I headed to London for the adventure of my life, and after doing the usual tourist bus trips, running out of money, then getting a job, I also found a husband. My first rescued cat came years later, after returning from a three-year sojourn overseas with my husband and two children.

We already had a cat and a dog, but I felt there was enough room and love in our home for another, especially one that was in desperate need.

It was close to Christmas and a sign had gone up at our local vet's: **'Pedigree Scottish Fold needs a new home urgently. No papers but friendly.'**

After ringing the number on the bottom of the notice, I heard the story of this poor little Scottish Fold. It seemed she was a present for a girlfriend but after numerous visits by the police and welfare officers, the occupants departed in a hurry leaving the little cat behind in the unit.

'Can you please feed the cat' was the message left for the next occupant of the unit.

Someone did feed her, but once again the occupants did a hasty exit when the police were called.

An elderly next-door neighbour had heard all the commotion, the fighting, the crashing of furniture and the departure of the occupants, and had wondered what had happened to the little Scottish Fold. It didn't take her long to hear her pitiful cries under a nearby shrub, but she was too frightened to venture out.

The neighbour started to put some food out for her but the little Fold cat was too scared to come out, especially as the food started to attract other neighbourhood cats. The neighbour then opened her laundry door and placed some food inside to encourage the cat to eat while she stood watching nearby. The cat would allow the lady to pat her but would then scurry outside to the safety of the shrub.

A few days later the elderly neighbour was taken away in an ambulance after suffering a heart attack. Her main worry, as told to her family, was who was going to look after the Scottish Fold cat she had been feeding. Hence the notice appearing at my local vet clinic.

It was close to Christmas and my husband had taken the train to work. He was attending a Christmas function and, being responsible, had decided not to drive. When we collected him from the station later that day, the children and I informed him that we were going to visit a cat that needed a home and was currently in someone's bathroom. It was a good time to announce a visit to a cat in desperate need, as my husband was merry and slightly intoxicated, and being a lover of cats, he somewhat readily agreed.

The elderly lady had returned home from hospital, accompanied by her daughter, and had captured the cat in the bathroom for us to visit.

There was no doubt this poor little cat had been through a lot. She was very skinny in spite of her long coat, and her big eyes were accentuated by the fold of her tiny ears. After gulping down her food she then came and sat by us, licking the remnants of food from her face as we gently stroked her. All of us were smitten and there was no doubt she thought being fed and having people fuss over her was what she was born for. The princess had found her forever home.

As a family we always chose a name we think fitted and then had a vote on it. Meggie was the name we had chosen and it seemed to suit her.

After arriving home with Meggie we set up a bed and litter tray in our room so that she would feel confident in her area of confinement. Having grown up in a very small flat, she was not used to a large house so we thought keeping her confined in our room would help her adjust more quickly.

Meggie was unsure of this arrangement and deposited herself inside my wardrobe when I had left it slightly ajar, wanting the comfort of the cave-like darkness. Moving a few shoes to accommodate her in her new cocoon, we then allowed her to go at her own pace.

Christmas Day had arrived and with it a 40°C hot day. We had spent many memorable Christmases in England and Europe with relatives and friends, wondering if it would snow on the day. Most times it didn't but the cold air with the grass crunching under our feet certainly raised an appetite. Christmas dinner in England is usually a feast to behold, starting with sherry or Gluhwein if someone had made it, while being teased with the enticing aromas emanating from the kitchen. We would then sit down to a meal of roast turkey or goose, ham, bread sauce, home-made cranberry sauce, lots of roasted winter vegetables and gravy. This was followed by plum pudding, brandy custard and cream, if you could fit it in. After lunch and the dishes done, we would all retire to play board games with the children while others slept it off by the fire.

In Australia on a 40°C plus day, most sensible people had cooked the turkey the day before on the barbeque outside, serving it up with lovely refreshing salads, or, as mostly happens today, have a feast of seafood and salads followed by pavlova.

Not in our household. We had the full English Christmas dinner, minus the bread sauce, followed by plum pudding and custard. I was exhausted.

The afternoon nap was strongly beckoning but first I cut a few pieces of cooked turkey and hand-fed them to my visitor in the wardrobe. After the first sniff, she gulped the meat down, then retreated back to the darkness and coolness of the wardrobe.

It was while I was in a state of dozing that I felt a rough tongue licking my hand, followed by a hot furry body nestling into the crook of my arm. Meggie had decided to join me on the bed and although we were both hot, I decided now was not the time to complain about it. She seemed so content lying there being gently stroked and having her funny little ears tickled. She must have been an expensive present for someone, and ending up homeless and starving is the last thing you would expect for such a sweet, pretty little girl.

Years later while working in rescue I came across a few pedigree cats who had somehow ended up homeless and neglected. I always wondered why someone would pay so much money to then throw them away, but then cats have always been seen as throwaway objects. Probably because they are carnivores and people think they can go and catch their own food if they want to eat.

Pedigree cats like Meggie are the antithesis of most cats. She wasn't a very bright cat and I sometimes wondered if there was anything going on between those folded-down ears. What Meggie lacked in brainpower and street smarts, she made up for with buckets of love. If anyone was upset, she would come over and place her paw on you, then place her head next to you as if she understood. She must have developed a strong sense of empathy after the despicable way she was treated. I grew to adore this funny little cat.

Meggie had decided that the wardrobe was no longer suitable as her lodgings, and our bed was to be her new domain. We agreed to appease her to start with, but having a hot, long-haired, affectionate cat snuggling into you on a hot night wasn't going to work. A cane chair with soft cushions around it was brought in and this became Meggie's chair. At first, she seemed offended by having a chair of her own, but we encouraged her to remain there while we tried to get a good night's sleep.

With her new-found status of being the queen of her chair in the master bedroom, Meggie would then tentatively explore the rest of the house. There was a Labrador dog who was pleasant enough but usually kept to himself, and another cat, a medium-haired tortoiseshell belonging to one of my daughters.

Meggie was not at all pleased about sharing her new abode with another cat and set about making her feelings known by extending her long fur and hissing loudly. Tammy, the resident cat, returned the favour by also extending her long fur and snarling in reply. Meggie the brave ran to the bedroom, and finding the wardrobe door now shut, jumped onto her chair, rolling herself into a ball, hoping no one – especially another cat – would find her.

It took a long time for the two cats to accept each other, and accept they barely did. Tammy was a confident cat who relished in having all the attention and she wasn't about to share it with some pretty interloper who arrived uninvited.

Meggie decided that the best strategy was to hiss at everything in her way until she arrived at her destination. She would quite often hiss at her own shadow leaving us all in fits of laughter at how silly she was. I really did start to believe there wasn't a lot going on between those ears.

One day Meggie surprised me and at the same time seemed to surprise herself. We had a long driveway and for her exercise she had followed me to the letterbox. When we were returning to the house, a Doberman from a neighbour's house appeared at the end of our drive and stood there, barking aggressively. With great concern I turned around to retrieve my cat, only to find she had turned herself into a large ball of fluff standing on four short legs, with a growl so loud and fierce that the dog stopped barking and hesitated. Meggie stood her ground, daring the dog to take one step further before being defaced by sharp claws and snarling teeth.

The dog took another look, decided retreating might be the best course of action, and ran off home from where he had come from. Watching the dog retreat I called Meggie back to me, but instead of strutting along with new-found pride in her stance, she zoomed past me at great speed, in through the cat flap and lay quivering under our bed. So much excitement for her to cope with in this new-found bravery had exhausted her. My hero slept for hours under the bed before returning to the safety of her chair.

The years rolled by with Meggie remaining princess of her domain on the cane chair. She never really ventured far, only to come for meals, and she preferred not to have hers at the same time as the other pets. Any kittens we were fostering were treated with the same disdain, and her strategy was to hiss first, ask questions later.

One summer day, an urgent noise emerged from one of the rooms. It was a cross between a loud squeak and an overly long high-pitched shriek. This was a sound I hadn't heard before so I was taken by surprise when I found out its source. Meggie had brought me a present and was proudly presenting me with a…moth. Her excitement at her captured prey had left the poor moth flapping around on the floor so I carefully scooped it up and placed it outside, much to her disgust. My gentle words of thanks seemed to be blocked by the flap over her ears because she stomped off back to her chair. It seems I was ungrateful for her efforts to help with the family dinner and a moth wasn't good enough for me. I don't think she ever forgave me because she never brought me any presents again.

Meggie passed away at 15 from renal failure. She had all the symptoms of kidney disease and a quick trip to the vet confirmed the kidneys were failing. Putting your pet to sleep is one of the hardest decisions you ever have to make and even vets will tell you it is so difficult when it is one of your own.

I have seen so much death and pain in rescue but losing one of your own, and in our case our first rescued cat, was so difficult. This funny little cat with the turned-down ears had won my heart and when she passed there was a gaping big hole left that seemed to be fathomless.

Meggie's cane chair remains in the bedroom, yet no other cat or kitten has claimed it for their own. It's as if the ghost of Meggie still remains and when I look at that chair, I sometimes think I still see her there with her big wide eyes and folded-down ears, hissing at shadows or her own reflection. How I miss that cat.

Joffrey – the Kitten Who Wanted to Live

A call came from a shelter that there were eight black and white kittens that had recently come in, and would we like them? After ascertaining their ages to be approximately 4 weeks, the ideal age to work on kittens and turn them into loving, affectionate pets, I readily accepted them.

After placing the eight kittens into the prepared bathroom, I then set about working with them to see how friendly they were. Eight sets of beady eyes widened when my hand approached, accompanied by a chorus of hissing and spitting, some of it enhanced by rushing at my hand. I was pretty certain they were feral kittens and put on gloves to save my hands from sets of tiny slashings.

In rescue we never know what we are dealing with when our little guests arrive and even the friendliest of kittens are often quite reticent until they know they are safe and no harm is going to come to them. Even with unknown or feral kittens, sometimes it only takes a few days for them to turn around, especially when they receive regular good food and warm words of encouragement. With these eight kittens it was a mixed reaction and some were quite ready to accept our hand of friendship while others had grave reservations.

If we had enough foster carers available, to speed up this process we often split the kittens up so we had more time for one-on-one work. We had family members, especially my teenage children, available to spend time with the kittens, and we chose those who we thought would be best together. There was one particular kitten my daughter called Joffrey who was the most difficult. I was quite keen to pass Joffrey on to the other foster carer but my daughter was up for the challenge of turning Joffrey around so, much to my disappointment, Joffrey remained with us.

Now, Joffrey was a special kitten, a bit smaller than the others and possibly the runt of the litter. He eyed me with the gravest suspicion, mustering up fiery spitballs anytime I approached him. With the safety of the gloves, I would pick him up by the scruff and with the other gloved hand would try to gently rub his back and around his ears. Joffrey was having none of it! He would hiss and squirm until I put him down again in defeat. He would then back up to the wall without taking his eyes off me and dare me to try doing that to him again, ready to hiss and spit as if his life depended on it. The wild glare in his eyes stated he was quite prepared to kill and eat me if it came to it. He won that round so I would retreat until the next day when we would try again.

I was becoming exasperated with Joffrey because his defiant hissy fits were not making it easy for the other three kittens to learn to trust us, and as soon as I thought we were

making progress, Joffrey would once again turn into a fluffy ball armed with needle-sharp claws. We needed to win him over so that he would keep quiet while we worked on the other kittens who were more receptive to our charms.

Food is often the way to a cat or kitten's heart and hand-feeding them some warm roast chicken often was the turning point in learning to trust. We would get them used to our hand coming to them with a tasty morsel so they would then be receptive to the hand touching their head and ears in gentle pats. Joffrey had other ideas and would snatch the piece of chicken from my hand and run off to some hidden corner to devour it. He was not falling for any of my tricks and he wasn't going to be party to any head rubs or ears being tickled.

As my daughter wanted Joffrey as a project to turn around, it was her duty to work on him. She would start

by forcing him to sit on her lap wrapped in a baby blanket with his head poking out so he couldn't escape. He would lie in this position having gentle pats forced on him, but there was a determined look in his eyes as if it were a battle of wills. He was a prisoner but the glare soon gave way to sleep. It was such an effort for a baby kitten to act so tough.

A phone call came out of the blue from the animal trainer Leeza Hura asking if we had any black and white kittens. As it was out of the normal kitten season, young kittens were in short supply, but I happened to have this feral litter who were just what she was after. A miniseries about INXS was being filmed and a black and white kitten was required for one of the music videos. Joffrey was the perfect candidate but there was just one problem. He was feral and not at all friendly. Leeza was not at all deterred by the problems I had with him and said she would work on him a few days before filming to get him used to being handled.

Arriving at the film studio, the kittens were all greeted by excited actors and crew. Joffrey had no choice but to be handled and in the green room between takes there was no shortage of actors or crew wanting to cuddle them. Joffrey's eyes widened at all the attention but he was beginning to get used to all the patting and cuddles, even enjoying it. He was slowly starting to come out of his shell.

Like all kittens, he quickly wore himself out, and in the expert hands of Leeza he soon forgot where he was and promptly fell asleep.

Joffrey and the other kittens were filmed for the series but, unfortunately for them, fame and fortune were left lying on the cutting room floor.

After a week of being cuddled and filmed, Joffrey and the other kittens returned home and we could see a marked difference in him. There was no more hissing, scratching or backing up against a wall ready to attack. He was still wide-eyed whenever a hand approached, but he was enjoying having his ears scratched and his chin tickled. He was still wary of me, but my daughter was making real progress with him. She would pick him up and then tuck him into her sweater, forcing him into a cocoon. They would watch TV together or do homework in this position. Being hidden in a sweater next to a beating warm heart was very soothing and soon this was Joffrey's favourite place to be. He could watch what was going on yet feel safe if he chose to sleep.

For weeks we worked on bringing Joffrey around to being friendly, but this stubborn little kitten had other ideas. He would happily play with his siblings, but as soon as they bounded up to us, he would just sit and observe.

One sunny winter's day we set up a temporary pen outside so they could get some fresh air and sunshine. This was a completely new experience for the kittens and after their first moments of fear they soon adjusted to it. First, they smelt the grass and savoured its flavour when they experimented in eating it. They would bounce around, sniffing the air, and watch in amazement at the leaves turning in the breeze or concentrate on a butterfly bouncing from weed to flower.

One of the great joys of fostering kittens is watching them develop new senses and play. They would bound around the pen, rolling over in play or chasing each other around. It was always entertaining and Joffrey was always in the thick of things, relishing the feel of grass under his paws. Three of the kittens would bound up for pats and it was at one of these times we saw the first signs of real progress with Joffrey. My daughter held her hand out to him and unexpectedly he started to headbutt it. This was the first indication we had had for weeks that he was starting to appreciate his foster home.

The kittens were soon up to the required weight for desexing and I felt they were ready for their forever homes. We would have to find a special home for Joffrey as he was still timid and he would need a home where they had the patience to keep working on him. The other kittens had completely turned around and were sweet, very affectionate, playful and ready to go.

The kittens were fitted with neck tags with their names and ages, then placed into the cat carrier before being taken to the vet for desexing.

After about an hour I received a phone call from the vet saying that the kitten named Joffrey had a category 5 heart murmur and his prognosis for living was very slim. He would most likely not make it past 6 months of age and did I want him euthanised while he was still at the clinic?

The news sent me spinning into shock. This was not what I expected and I had to make a decision on the spot about his life. It was a decision I just couldn't make – ending a life is always hard and we would only do it if the animal was likely to be put through great pain and suffering.

Joffrey seemed so normal, so healthy. I wasn't prepared for this news.

Thinking quickly, I asked to vet to hold off while I made some calls. My daughter, who had placed so much effort and love in turning Joffrey around, would be devastated. It would break her heart, she would be inconsolable, and as a family we would all be distraught. If I brought him home, at least he would be able to spend his last days with us loving and caring for him, plus it would give us all a chance to say goodbye.

With a heavy heart I collected the groggy kittens, and the very alert Joffrey, and brought them home. The vet fully understood my dilemma. If Joffrey started to deteriorate, I would bring him back to the surgery so he wouldn't suffer for long.

The family were as shocked as I was about the terrible news and vowed that we would do everything possible to give him the life he deserved before he passed on.

'That will teach me to name him after a *Game of Thrones* character who gets killed off,' my daughter said, sobbing. We all felt numb with the sorrow of what was to come.

The other kittens were all rehomed and Joffrey remained, being treated like royalty in his last days with us. He looked so well, played like a normal kitten, ate like a normal kitten and continued to grow more attached to my daughter. He loved the special treatment he was receiving but he still kept a wary eye on me.

With his siblings gone, Joffrey established a friendship with Imp, who was my daughter's cat. Imp was an orphan who came to us with a sibling at 1 week old, having been found abandoned in a flowerpot. They were taken to a vet clinic and we got a call asking if we had a mother cat who could take them on. We did, so we rushed to the clinic as time was critical for kittens this age.

Having been left in a flowerpot, the tiny babies had snuffled through the dirt looking for a milky teat. They were in quite a filthy state and getting them respectably clean for a mother to take on was quite a task. On top of that they had extremely loud lungs for 1-week-olds and our journey home was accompanied by a chorus of desperate and hungry crying.

As an older kitten, Imp was a beautiful surrogate mother who lavished love and affection on the grateful Joffrey. He adored her and followed her wherever she went.

Six months rolled by and Joffrey still looked healthy and was behaving like a normal kitten. Another appointment was made for the vet to check him over to see how he was

developing and whether the heart murmur was still prominent. It was still there but Joffrey wasn't showing any symptoms of worsening; in fact, he was quite the opposite.

Our vet recommended we have him desexed and see if he could handle the anaesthetic. If he came through the operation, he could live a bit longer but we didn't know for how long.

The day came for his desexing operation and with a looming dread we brought Joffrey into the vet clinic. Our cuddles, followed by long goodbyes, were tainted with the knowledge that we might not see him again. His heart may not be strong enough to cope with the anaesthetic.

The hours slowly ticked by until it was time to collect our little boy and bring him home, or so we hoped. No one from the vet clinic had called so we assumed he had come through his operation and his heart had held firm. The vet was as pleased as us that all had gone well, but the category 5 heart murmur remained. After a lengthy explanation about what may be next, he then recommended we visit the animal heart specialist for further examination and analysis. There was only one heart specialist in Melbourne and the cost would be significantly more than the normal veterinary rate. As a cat rescue, our funds were limited and spending so much on one kitten, who in all probability wouldn't survive for long, made it a hard decision.

My daughter, however, had no hesitation in withdrawing the required amount from her savings so an appointment was then made.

It wasn't long before the visit to the heart specialist arrived so my daughter gently placed Joffrey into the cat carrier for his big day. We would know one way or another whether he was going to survive and for how long.

It was explained to the vet staff on the phone that Joffrey was a feral kitten but we had been working on him and making excellent progress. The specialist vet eyed Joffrey with a practised but suspicious eye and wondered how a feral kitten would take to being put on a heart monitor and having an ultrasound. I'm sure he had visions of going home with his arms wrapped in blood-soaked bandages.

Joffrey was placed over a table with my daughter holding his front legs while I held the back legs. His whole body began to shake as the fur was shaved from around his heart and the cold gel for the ultrasound was smoothed over the newly shaven fur. He didn't struggle or move while the specialist glided the monitor over his heart – he was just too terrified.

After about 15 minutes the ordeal was over. While the specialist went into another room to examine the results, we relaxed our hold on Joffrey who then placed his paws around my daughter's neck. He clung to her so tightly that the gel from the ultrasound left her shirt with an imprint of a squashed cat.

The specialist took time to explain to us what was happening to Joffrey and that only time would tell if it was to be good news or bad.

He had a hole in his heart but the hole was small enough for the blood to flow quickly past. Whether this remained or closed up as he got older would determine if he lived and for how long. He still had a heart murmur but it was a category 3, not a 5 as first suspected.

After bringing Joffrey home it was decided that we would keep him to see how he developed, and whether he would live a normal life. He certainly seemed normal as he continued to show affection to my daughter and occasionally to me. He idolised Imp and followed her around, waiting for her to show him a scrap of affection. Imp was in charge and like many cats with a bit of power she tossed bits of affection his way when it suited her. Whenever Imp decided it was naptime, Joffrey would curl up with her and embrace the moment like a lovestruck teen.

In the foster home, kittens came and went, with Joffrey always being ready to play, but as he got older and bigger, he soon tired of the same antics. He was part of the family so showed his superiority by playing rough, resulting in him being separated from the little kittens. He still adored Imp and followed her wherever she went, until Imp tired of him and sent him scurrying with a swipe of her paw or a growl.

A few years later Joffrey became very ill. He had a high temperature and his breathing was heavy. From all the reading and researching we had done since seeing the heart specialist, we knew that his prognosis wasn't good and that he could depart from this world at any time.

A quick trip to the vet confirmed our worst fears, but to make Joffrey comfortable he was given antibiotics and medication.

We fussed over our dear little feral boy, as we affectionately called him, and made sure he was as comfortable as possible. He lay in the cat bed, barely raising a sleepy eye

when we came near. His temperature was starting to come down as the antibiotics kicked in and his heavy breathing started to wane.

We knew rest was also the best medicine for Joffrey so kept checking for signs of change. He started to look more pert, so food was offered to him. Knowing this could be his last meal with us, we gave him all the treats he liked and a selection of different foods to tempt him. All the time we took turns in sitting with him, stroking his ears and telling him what a good boy he was. Joffrey was enjoying all this attention being bestowed on him. If these were to be his last minutes with us, we wanted to be sure he had all the love we could give.

After about a week of this special care, when it seemed Joffrey was going to pull through, we took him back to the vet's for another check-up. The fluid in his lungs had cleared up, his temperature was normal and he was back to eating regular food with a few extra treats for good measure.

With the vet shaking his head in amazement at Joffrey's turnaround and our excitement at having our feral boy a bit longer, life carried on as normal.

More foster kittens came and went over the year, with Joffrey playing with the older ones who were up for a game of tussle.

Imp had departed the family home along with my daughter to their new residence, so Joffrey, now around 3 years old, had a new-found status in the house. He continued to show us affection but still had a skittishness about him. He would jump at any noise he was unfamiliar with and hide under a couch until he thought the danger had subsided.

Along with his affection there were still remnants of the feral cat inside him.

About a year later Joffrey again succumbed to a high temperature, lethargy, no appetite and difficulty breathing. With temperatures over 41°C our worst fears reappeared so he was rushed back to the vet's for an examination, more medicine and antibiotics.

There was no doubt Joffrey was a very sick boy but this time extra tests were done to see if there was some other underlying problem other than his heart defect.

Again, Joffrey was nursed with the utmost care, having love and affection showered on him. Our little feral boy would want for nothing as we soothed his head with gentle pats. Our reward was the soft purring as he slept. If his heart was about to give up, then our boy would know that his family loved him very much.

The temperature eventually came down, his appetite returned and slowly Joffrey turned the corner. Once again, we became hopeful that we would have him for a bit longer.

The test results came back, with our vet looking a little perplexed at the information they contained. The results were inconclusive, but it seemed his illness wasn't a result of his failing heart. Whatever it was, Joffrey had fought it off and was starting to look the picture of health. It was possible one of the previous foster kittens had passed an illness on to him but we would never really know. It didn't really matter because our feral boy was still with us.

I had jokingly come to my own conclusion about what had ailed Joffrey. He had 'Man Flu' or ASI, 'attention seeking illness'. He just loved being the centre of attention, especially now that Imp had left. Being fussed over, having his ears and chin gently scratched, having his food brought to his bed so he didn't have to stretch too far were all cures for this illness. In reality it was probably the antibiotics that brought his illness under control and thankfully his heart would keep beating for a bit longer.

A few years later we sold our house and moved to our new home, bringing our pets with us. At first Joffrey was confined to the bathroom for a few days while our furniture and possessions were placed in their new surrounds. He had a cocoon bed where he could hide away, uncertain about why everything familiar had been taken away from him. When it was time for our evening meal, we would allow him out to sniff his way around his new home, always pausing by something familiar as if to give him some reassurance of his life before.

It wasn't long before Joffrey settled into our new home, with new smells and noises becoming familiar and not so scary. He carried on without a care in the world.

He is getting old now and starting to slow down in the way cats of this age do. His heart is still beating strongly so we can only assume that the hole in his heart has grown over with time, as the specialist said it might. Just occasionally he gives us a scare when he coughs and splutters, often when he is purring loudly, as if there is a permanent furball lodged in his throat. We will watch him until he catches his breath and his breathing goes back to being normal.

There are still elements of the feral cat in him, especially when there is a new noise or someone comes to visit. At those times he is a black and white flash as he makes a dash for safety underneath the bed or sofa. He will only resurface when he feels his cocoon of normality returning and the clanging of the feed bowl at mealtime soon brings his reality back. He winds between legs and rubs up against familiar furnishings as if there had been no disturbance to his daily routine, his Jekyll-and-Hyde personality swinging back to that of a loving friendly cat. With his belly full and in the safety of his fluffy bed, he pummels the sides as if he is stamping through a sticky syrup.

'You are one very lucky boy,' I tell him as he sleepily raises one eye before lulling himself off to sleep with a soft purr.

I think he agrees with me.

Bella – the Journey of an Angry Cat

It was the usual phone call: a litter of six kittens had come into the shelter and do we want to take them? We always try to fit kittens into our rescue program and these ones at 5 to 6 weeks old were the perfect age as they could feed and toilet themselves, were into play and would quickly learn to socialise in a family home.

Checking to see what supplies I would need for six hungry kittens, I then laid a fluffy blanket into a cat carrier and headed off to the shelter.

The kittens were in an isolation room, so when I arrived I went straight into the cattery to see what other cats had come in over the past week.

There was the usual array of cats, some who came straight up to the front of the cage as if to say, 'I really don't belong in here. Please would you take me home?' to the ones who were hiding at the back of the cage awaiting their fate, or others still who were sniffing or munching on kibble and giving me just a cursory glance.

There was one in particular who caught my attention. She was a very pretty blue and cream cat who was sitting at the back of the cage and didn't show any interest in what I was doing at all.

One of the staff pointed to her and said, 'This cat has a sad story.' I was always interested to hear about the background of any cats who came in and had seen and heard about many tragic cases before. It always helps to know a little about the cats' history so we can plan the recovery process.

This cat had come from a drug addict's house and what the rangers saw when they entered the house was horrific. There were several animals at the property, dogs and other cats, all in a sad state of emaciation. There were several dead kittens on the floor, all supposedly belonging to the blue and cream cat now sitting at the back of the cage.

It was easy to understand her lack of interest in her surroundings, but from what the staff said, when it came to food she was food aggressive, in other words she was in starvation mode. She would growl as she ate her food, grabbing the bowl with her paws and dragging it to the back of the cage like a devil possessed. After eating she would then return to her place at the back of the cage with total lack of interest in the goings on of the shelter. She was so thin that her bones stuck out at angles, making her look deformed, and her eyes had the dullness of a depression that could only come from seeing things no animal should ever see, or worse, endure.

I was chatting with the staff when six squawking baby kittens were brought into the cattery, and as with all babies we gathered around to admire them. There were five tabbies and one ginger one, probably a throwback from the past or perhaps a different dad. They were adorable and I could see from their health and age that these babies would settle very well in foster care and be highly sought after.

It was at this stage that I noticed a change in the little mother cat. Her ears shot up, and her eyes sharpened as she focused on the high-pitched, squeaky mews of the kittens. She stood up and came to the front of the cage for a closer look, then settled back, alert and watching.

The kittens became increasingly loud with incessant meows and when one of the staff members picked up one of the tabbies and held it close to her, the kitten burst into a song of loud purring.

The little cat watched intently, taking in all that was happening to this kitten. 'Let's put the kitten in with this little cat as I think she still has some milk,' I said to the staff member, 'and if she accepts it, we may have a mother to look after them.'

We placed the baby in the front of the cage and waited to see what would happen. If it didn't go well, I would be able to open the cage and grab the kitten before any damage was done. This would be unusual, as mother cats usually have a strong mothering instinct, but we didn't know what this little cat had been through so we were dealing with the unknown. It's always best to be cautious.

The kitten ran straight up to the cat and started nuzzling for a teat. We anxiously waited to see what her reaction would be and whether she would accept this little hungry mouth.

At first she pulled back to get a good look at the little tabby, then started sniffing. Obviously it didn't smell like her own baby but she was interested. She started to lick its face which I knew was a good sign, then promptly lay down to allow the baby to latch on to a teat. Whether she had enough milk to feed six babies was questionable but I knew that with good food brought to her often, and lots of love and gentleness, she would soon start to produce enough for the hungry kittens.

We then loaded the five remaining kittens into the carrier, adding the test one after, and put the little cat into a separate carrier. We didn't want things to go badly on the journey home so to be safe we had to keep them separated. We would then try the same process again in the room I had prepared for their arrival. This was going to be easy, or so I thought. Our new little babies had a mother to look after them and I had saved the life of this little cat.

After opening the carrier door containing the kittens and allowing them to sniff their new surroundings, I then opened the other carrier door for the little skinny cat and waited to see her reaction. She stepped out cautiously but her interest in her new surroundings was overtaken by her interest in the kittens. She still wasn't sure of them, even after they ran to her in search of milk. She took several steps back, wanting to sniff them in case they were her own babies but her curiosity was still piqued. This was make-or-break time.

It was time to name the little cat and the name Violet

sprang to mind due to her unusual colours. She had a lot of grey with blue tones which meant a Russian Blue or British Blue may have been in her genes, along with any other variation for the cream. She was a true Moggie with a regal look that was accentuated by how skeletal she was.

After sniffing the babies and realising her new surroundings were safe, Violet lay down to allow her new brood to nuzzle into her, searching for the teats. This was a great beginning and I left the room with happy thoughts of giving this poor depressed cat back some babies. She was happy, the babies were happy and so was I.

The first thing to do after settling any new cat and her brood into a room was to make sure the mother had plenty of food and water. Violet was so skinny that her teats protruded, making her look out of proportion. If she was to take on six hungry babies, I would need to build her milk supply up and that meant plenty of food. As she hadn't been

in the shelter for long, I was unsure about what food she was accustomed to and there was always a risk of her developing diarrhoea. We always gave flea and worm treatments as well, so that was also a contributing factor to having stomach upsets. That would make for a very difficult time for a nursing mother, which would also be reflected in the babies as it was something that could take at least a week to settle.

At the age of 6 weeks the babies should be weaning off the mother and eating by themselves so with this in mind I prepared a small amount of kitten food to see if they would start on solids. Because Violet was so undernourished, she would also be given kitten food as the nutrients in it would help to build her strength back up plus build the milk supply.

Armed with the bowls of food I entered the room and put it down before my new guests. What happened next threw my well-laid plans out the window. In a fit of rage Violet pounced on the bowls of food, snarling as she ploughed through their contents, with the kittens escaping in all directions for cover. She was aggressively hungry, as if this were her last meal and nobody or nothing was going to get in the way.

Nothing had quite prepared me for her reaction to food, and scattering the kittens with her snarling was not quite what I had planned for our happy family. She was going to be a problem and I was starting to regret bringing her along with the kittens.

The kittens were at the age where they should be socialised, happy to interact with humans and snuggle up with the foster family. Violet had other plans. She would gather the kittens into her as if to protect them from the enemy within the room – me.

From Violet, the kittens were learning to fear humans and that they were not to be trusted. I couldn't get near them without her giving me a warning that she would not tolerate me touching them. I had to win her over first and that was going to take time, time I didn't have much of if I was going to have the babies ready for adoption at around 10 weeks of age.

Winning over an animal is usually done with food, gentle talking and lots of love. Violet was no exception, although she had changed the rules slightly. Whenever I took the food bowls in, the angry food aggression began, but the length of time it went on for was starting to reduce. She was getting the right nourishment and being fed three times a day, and of course cats love routine. This was a routine she adapted to very well and slowly her coat began to take on a glossier tone and her eyes became brighter. It may have been my imagination but her angular, starved body was also becoming more rounded, all positive signs. She was also allowing the babies to feed out of the bowls but wanted them close to her while keeping a wary eye on what I was doing.

This was my time to work on her so I started by not going in too close but getting her used to my voice. I would tell her what a beautiful girl she was, what a clever mother she was to take on these babies and how sad she must have been to have lost her own babies. Like any female, she loved being told she was beautiful, and slowly I would scratch her behind the ears, ever so gently. Violet would always jerk her head up to see what I was about to do, then surrendered her ears to my gentle touch. I would continue to do that while she happily ate and a trust between us began.

The kittens had taken to eating solids with gusto, perhaps because Violet didn't have enough milk to go around. At this age it wasn't so important, and nestling on a teat was more a comfort thing for both mother and kittens.

After a few days, the hunger growling stopped and the kittens were no longer afraid when I entered the room with the food bowls. They would start to tumble and play like normal kittens and Violet would often sit up high on the cat tree while watching them. She still had a distance in her eyes, a cloud of depression almost as if she were in another land, another space. Perhaps she was and maybe she was pinching herself to see if this was real. Perhaps she was still mourning the loss of her own babies or reflecting on the life she had before. An air of caution around me remained and she would gather the babies in for protection. I still had work to do to win her trust.

I've hardly ever had a cat that didn't love a roast and I used a Sunday lamb roast to start the next stage of winning Violet over. I would cut small pieces of lamb from the family dinner and hand-fed these to her. It seemed she had never smelt or tasted lamb roast before, and as I held a piece close to her nose, her senses were instantly aroused. She would come and sniff the meat, then open her mouth to snatch the morsel away. This new taste pleased her as I knew it would and she'd hurriedly come back for more. Piece by piece I hand-fed her, with her licking her lips after each mouthful. It was working. While doing this I kept telling her what a beautiful girl she was and how good she was to look after the babies.

The next stage beyond gentle ear scratches was full body stroking. Violet was now in charge – how would she react? She could have slapped my hand away with her outstretched paw, recoiled at my touch and hid, or elongated her body to extend the stretch. Fortunately for me she chose the latter so the elongated body stretch was the lesson for the day.

Food, gentle talking and now stroking. This was a really good sign but there was still a cautiousness in her eyes which told me she wasn't ready for a full surrender to my charms.

After a couple of weeks, Violet became used to me coming into the room. With her new-found addiction to roast meat, I experimented with different meats, which raised her expectation of new taste sensations. Every time the routine was the same: I would hand-feed her while gently talking to her, then she would allow me to stroke her. While this was going on the kittens were coming up to see what Mumma was eating. They were no longer afraid of me coming into the room with food bowls and now started to look forward to the twice daily ritual.

After starting them on baby kitten food, I then progressed to a more adult taste and the kittens loved it. I interspersed it with meat from the roast and some raw mince, and I could see the healthy glow appear in their shiny coats and eyes. It was now time for play and socialising.

Sitting down on the floor with a feathery toy on a stick, I would wave it around to gain their attention and soon they were jumping up in anticipation of the reward of capture.

Through running the feathers over my legs, the kittens were starting to sit on my lap, waiting for their chance to lunge as the toy swept by. This was getting them used to me and gave me the opportunity to tickle their tummies or stroke their ears. They were learning that touch from a human could be soothing and fun and they particularly loved lying upside down so I could give them the belly rub they enjoyed. A kitten or cat lying on its back and exposing its vulnerable side to you is a sign of complete trust and this is part of the training we do to get them used to being handled.

Violet would often sit up high on the study bench under the window or on the cat tree and watch everything that was happening in her now safe world. Her demeanour was changing from wide-eyed alertness to relaxed dreamy-eyed calmness. She was content with her lot, and raising these babies in the foster home had meant the horrors of the past were slipping into her distant memory, something I was aiming for.

It was during this time that other members of the family would come and play with the kittens or give them cuddles. We also carried on the ritual of hand-feeding pieces of roast meat to Violet so she didn't give preference to only one person feeding her. She still wouldn't let us hold her, and if we tried, she returned an angry look that warned us not to try again. She was happy and content so long as we didn't try to move her. Getting her into a cat carrier to take her to the vet was going to be a problem so I had to work out a strategy to ease her into this new move.

The kittens were progressing very well and would soon be up to a kilo in weight and ready for their vet work. Violet was still the doting mother, but with the kittens at the age of 8 weeks or more it was like having a room full of teenagers.

If Violet sat up high on the bench or the cat tree, the kittens would try and jump up to catch her tail. Violet, annoyed by this, would swish her tail back and forth, which would only encourage the kittens more. She would often let out a sigh and swish her tail up higher so it was out of reach of those sharp little claws. This would only encourage the kittens to try even harder and if a claw did reach flesh, Violet would let out a growl and move further out of reach. She had so much patience, but there were limits and she let the kittens know it.

Some cats are born mothers and adopt anything that moves on four legs, mothering and nurturing with an ancient instinct embedded in them. Other mothers, usually first-time, very young mothers, are quick to dispense with motherly instinct duties and don't want a bar of their fun-loving, naughty babies. These are usually the mothers who never had time to be kittens or behave in a kittenish way before falling pregnant and being lumped with the responsibilities of babies. Quite often when their mothering duties are finished, they return to being a kitten and make up for lost time. This is especially the case once they have been desexed and the calling of nature to reproduce has ceased. For them it is 'me' time.

The kitten socialising was progressing nicely and it didn't take long before they made a fast bolt through the open door of their room. Often, they would zoom out, then screech to a halt and hesitate, thinking, 'What now?' Tentatively they'd venture a bit further but were always ready to race back to the safety of their own room. Being naturally curious creatures, the kittens would continue further into the larger family room and start to explore. Violet would come out as well, anxious in case the kittens ran into any danger, always ready to spring to their defence. She wouldn't come into the family room but would sit in the short passageway and observe. If she spotted one of our own cats, she was determined not to give them any cause for complaint and would sit quietly but ready to exit back to the safety of her own room if needed.

Every day when the kittens were let out they would venture further into the family room, taking possession of any area left vacant by the dog and resident cats. The kittens thought this was great fun and started to become more adventurous in coming up to the resident pets. This was when new toys were brought out and the energetic kittens would chase after the ping pong ball under the couch, or the mouse going around in circles on the electric machine.

They would often come to see what I was doing and try to join in. If I was mopping the floor, they had to have a look in the bucket to see what was making the soft sploshing noise. Chasing after the mop was great fun and the kitten who could surf on top while it whizzed around the floor felt so superior, until, that is, it fell over, rolling to a halt.

This is the fun part of raising kittens and as a family we enjoyed the interaction with them and the inevitable curl up on the lap when exhaustion took over. It is hard not to fall in love with these little bundles of energy and every day with them was cherished as we knew it wouldn't last.

Violet had now started to come further into the family

room while these kitten shenanigans were going on, always observing and occasionally licking a passing kitten. She would sometimes hold them down roughly, giving them a sound grooming, while the squirming kitten tried to escape. This made her hold them down harder if she had not finished washing their faces and backs and nothing would deter her from finishing the ablutions. Like all small kids and kittens, there was a bit of resentment at this treatment and once released the kitten would bound away again distracted by the next thing to capture its fancy.

If I was sitting at the table working or reading, Violet would often come and sit at my feet, content to be near me but not so near that she couldn't escape back to her own room. She had now come to trust me and still loved getting her pieces of roast meat hand-fed, supplemented by the regular food she was receiving. Instead of the wide-eyed, cautious stare, her eyes would form soft slits and she would blink in happiness. Violet was quite a different cat now and I was starting to fall in love with her. She had come such a long way, but getting her into a cat carrier was still an issue as she would not allow me to pick her up. Having her feet firmly on the ground gave her security and a means of escape should she need it. She was not ready to forgo that and would not allow herself to be held.

Getting Violet into the cat carrier was my next task because the kittens were ready to go to the vet and Violet had to go too. I brought in the carrier, with a little blanket inside, and left it on the bench with the door open. Violet recoiled when she saw the carrier and started hissing at the open door. It was going to be difficult to get her into it and I didn't want her reverting to hiding and growling.

Leaving the door open and the carrier where it was, I then set about playing with the kittens, ignoring Violet who was still eyeing the carrier with all the suspicion of an angry snake charmer. She finally stepped back from it, although keeping a wary eye on it, to check what the babies were doing. When it seemed the carrier posed no immediate threat, she retreated to the cat tree to watch the kittens as they played and tumbled with each other, and darted all over the room in a game of chase.

I left the room, with the kittens racing out the door to catch me, and the little bundles of energy headed off in all directions to see what the resident cats and dog were up to. Violet was left with the carrier for company as I knew she had to get used to it being a piece of room furniture.

The next day was weighing day so each kitten was placed on the scales to see if they had reached a kilo in weight. It was hard to keep each wriggling body still enough to take a reading, but when the dial went over the mark they could be booked in for their vet work, when they would be microchipped, vaccinated and desexed.

As we were a rescue organisation, vet work was automatic for each cat or kitten that came through us, done at this young age so they recovered quickly and their stitches were minimal. Usually by the next morning, after feeling groggy and sorry for themselves, the males would be back to their energetic selves although sometimes the females took a little longer to recover.

With the kittens booked into the vet, they had their extra last feed at 10 pm and then all food and water was taken from the room.

Violet had become used to the carrier with the door open and no longer viewed it as the black hole. She had to go into the carrier first and then the kittens would be gathered up, with their name tags placed around their necks so the vet knew which kitten was which. I had to act fast.

With all the name tags done and another carrier on standby outside the door, I opened the door to the room, quickly closing it behind me to stop escaping bundles of fluff. The kittens had become used to me coming at this time of day with their breakfast so they were quite eager stay in their room instead of trying their usual escape antics.

Violet was also excited because this time of day meant food, and although she no longer fought for it, it was still the highlight of her day. After placing the name tags on the table, I then ventured close to the open carrier where Violet would come for her usual ear scratch and stroking. She was totally trusting of me now and quite relaxed through all the soothing words and gentle touch.

Quick as a flash and with her body in the right position I grabbed her by the scruff of her neck and shoved her into the carrier, closing the door after her. Violet was in shock, feeling utterly betrayed by my actions, and the dilated pupils in her eyes reappeared. This time instead of showing anger she looked hurt, as if her whole world had come crashing down.

Gathering the kittens one by one, I then placed the name tags around their necks and settled them in the waiting carrier by the door. Instead of their usual chatter of mini meows, there was silence, as they were unsure of what was happening to them.

After placing the babies in the back seat of the car, I then put Violet in the front beside me and turned the carrier so she could look at me. She looked painfully thin again, crouching at the back of the carrier, wondering why her safe little world had suddenly disappeared. I could only imagine what was going through her mind and no doubt flashes of her horrible past where she was abused and starved would have been racing through her mind. Keeping my eyes on the road I tried to soothe her with kind words, but I could see she was shaking. Poor darling little girl. I vowed then that I would find the very best home for her when the time came, for I had grown so very fond of this dear little half-starved cat, now looking so distraught and fearful.

During the afternoon I was clock watching, waiting for the time to pass so I could collect Violet and the kittens and bring them back to the safety of their own room.

I gently placed the carriers down and opened the doors to let the little family back into their familiar surroundings. They were still groggy from the anaesthetic. Violet went and hid under the bench, away from the babies, sore and feeling sorry for herself.

Sometimes upon returning from the vet's a sore but usually doting mother cat can turn on her babies, hissing and snarling at them. They smell of anaesthetic, vet clinic smells and everything foreign that reminds them of the trauma they have recently been through. The shocked little babies would crawl off to a place away from Mumma and usually take comfort in each other while sleeping the experience off.

This is usually the time the family take it in turns to cuddle the sleepy kittens, allowing them to snuggle up in contentment, knowing that we love them. If we have a timid kitten, this is often a great way to create a bond, and often when they recover from the surgery they come up for more cuddles and attention.

By the next morning appetites have usually returned and mothers are back licking and loving their babies. Violet was no different. She fussed over them, smelling and licking off the reminders of the vet visit. She would also lie down to give them a comforting feed of milk, but now the kittens were so big that it didn't usually last for long and she would suddenly jump up and out of their way. Kittens this age have sharp little teeth and sometimes they use them to nip the teat to stimulate the milk, much to the mother's displeasure.

These adorable little kittens recovered quickly and it was soon time to put them up for adoption. It was also time to think about getting a home for Violet – that was going to be a challenge. I had become so fond of this little cat and she was doting on me.

She came to us in such a sad state of neglect, so skinny her bones stuck out, and with a depression that had aged her more than her 18 months of barely living. Would there be someone out there who would continue Violet's journey to recovery and trust? Would she ever forgive me for betraying the trust she had in me when I passed her on to someone else? I put these thoughts out of my mind. I would worry about it when the time came. It was now time to find homes for the babies.

Each of the kittens had a photo taken and a short description written of their personality for our Facebook and web page, in adoptions. In a way it was hard to write a description as all six had such gorgeous natures and of course they were all very pretty with their tabby markings. There are only so many times you can write adorable, sweet-natured, playful, perfect. As I expected, applicants wanting them came quickly, and when the last kitten went off to their forever home, it was just Violet left behind.

Violet had been such a devoted attentive mother to the babies, I was wondering how she would react to not having them around. At first, she called them, going from room to room to see if they had disappeared on one of their adventures around the house. When no kittens answered her call, she would quietly settle near me, often on the chair next to where I was sitting.

She was such an easy cat to have around and seemed content to be in my company but never posing a threat to my own pets. They would look at her with an air of superiority but she ignored them, just happy to be part of the family. If I was working at the kitchen table, she would sit on the chair looking at me in a content state of bliss. This is what she yearned for, everything she ever wanted, a safe and happy home where she would never go hungry again and have kind words spoken to her.

If I ever had to raise my voice at one of my own pets, Violet would run to the refuge of the kitten room, afraid in case she had upset me, her place of safety shattered. She was so sensitive to her surroundings and grateful for the home I was giving her that I'm sure she would have done backflips on her tail had I asked it. She wanted to please me, to make sure I would never leave her as had happened to her so many months ago.

I had put up many posts on our rescue Facebook page about Violet and her babies which meant many people had learnt her story – coming from a terrible situation to adopting the babies, her transition from being a starving angry cat to a gentle loving one. I had built up a picture of Violet, hoping someone would want to take her home and give her the love she deserved.

I knew parting with her was going to be one of the most difficult things I'd ever have to do. Violet would feel abandoned again, but if she was to have a permanent and loving home, it was a pain she would have to endure. I had to find someone who had the patience and willingness to make Violet feel loved and safe. Who would take on this role? Who would help Violet continue her journey from being an angry cat to a devoted and loving cat?

By now, Violet was looking like the pretty, sleek blue and cream girl she was meant to be. Her body was still angular and small but there was a glow in her fur, a light in her eyes and a brightness in her demeanour. Grabbing the camera, I managed to capture this image while she was sitting on the chair next to me and

I set about writing up a piece on our Facebook page that I hoped would attract the right person or people who would love her as much as I had grown to love her.

Peninsula Cat Rescue Inc.

November 27, 2014

We are now looking for a special home for Violet. In what has possibly been the worst case of neglect we have come across, this 18-month little lady came into foster care and adopted six hungry, noisy little orphans. Violet is a special case in that her distrust of humans means she will need the right home and we are looking for someone who will give her the time and space to continue her journey to recovery. She has come a long way and the way to her heart is through food. With time and patience, we are fairly certain this pretty young cat will turn into a loving, friendly, affectionate pet. If you are up to the challenge and think you are right for Violet then please contact Joy.

It was always a delight to hear from my friend Elise and even more remarkably delightful to hear that she wanted the challenge of taking on Violet by offering her a permanent home. I couldn't believe my luck.

I never know who is going to call me with a view to adopting a kitten or a cat, but this call was out of the blue. Elise is a writer, a published author who would be at her desk sometimes for hours, researching, reading and writing. She wanted to take on the challenge of Violet and she had the time to devote to her. Violet would be her companion and reading mate, a match made in heaven. I was so excited, and when I told the family who wanted Violet, none of us could think of a better home for her to go to. And as an added bonus, I would still get to see her.

As Elise is my friend, I decided to take Violet to her and help her get settled in. There would be some advice she would need to take on board and the same approach I had taken would need to be continued in her new home.

Violet was still eating her breakfast when I brought the carrier into the kitten room. I placed it quietly on the bench in the hope she wouldn't notice.

Not on your life. Quick as a flash she abandoned her bowl, very unusual for her, and firmly wedged herself under the bench on a plastic box. She was not going to be tricked or fooled into going into the carrier again and a determined streak flashed across her eyes. Even bits of food dangled in front of her nose were not going to budge her – she was not falling for that old chestnut. How was I going to get her into the carrier with no room to get a good hold on her or even to scruff her neck? I'd thought she would go in easily now we'd established a bond of trust, but trust with a cat had its limits and Violet had come to the end of hers.

I abandoned the room with the view of coming back later when she was back at the food bowl and more relaxed, so I was disappointed when I returned after an hour or so to find Violet still in her protected spot. I had to try and dislodge her from this position, scruff her neck and quickly lift her into the carrier, and for this I needed reinforcements. Other members of the family joined in, trying to coax Violet out of her security cave. She eyed us all with great suspicion and I was afraid she would revert to her swiping action, claws out to attach to some flesh.

With all the extra distractions around I was able to slip my hand in from behind and scruff her neck while trying to slip my other hand under her body and pull her out. She resisted but there were no claws, no swiping or growling, just strong resistance. I could understand her reluctance to leave the security of her room, but I had a much better one for her to go to, one where she didn't have to compete with the resident cats, one where she could be queen of her own castle because it was her new permanent loving home.

After loading the carrier into the car, I set off for Elise's house with Violet looking at me through the wire door of the cage in complete bewilderment. Why was I doing this when she had been so good? Why was I taking her away? I tried to reassure her that she was going to a place where she would be the only cat, where she would have all the attention she ever wanted, and of course plentiful food. All of this seemed to fall on deaf ears. Violet was not at all convinced and she retreated to the back of the carrier to await her fate.

A happy and excited greeting met us when Elise opened the door to guide us into the living room. We closed a few doors around the house, leaving the main room for Violet to explore with us there to reassure her.

At first, she sat at the back of the carrier, but then her curiosity got the better of her and she ventured out. Violet's first few steps were done in crouching mode, but then realising there was lots to investigate and new smells to entice her, she began to explore. Her nose twitched as she moved from the sofa to the floor. To continue the journey of trust, I had suggested to Elise that she have some ready supplies of cooked chicken or treats to win her over with.

After an hour or more of exploring, with Elise and I watching out of the corner of our eyes, it was time for me to return home. I left Elise with instructions to call me if there were any problems. It is always a relief when one of our mother cats finds a loving home, but with Violet, I knew Elise would have a challenge in winning her trust and it wouldn't be straightforward. I knew it would take a few days for Violet to settle, so even though I wanted to know how Violet was going, I had to let it go. With fostering and running a cat rescue there were always other pressing issues to occupy my mind, but that didn't stop me wondering and worrying. In this case, no news was good news.

The first thing Elise did was rename Violet to Bella and Bella really did suit this feisty little cat.

At first Bella hid under the sofa and she did a pretty good job of concealing herself there. It took Elise many frustrating hours worrying if she had inadvertently left the door open, wondering if there was a window slightly ajar, or had Bella somehow got out without Elise seeing where she went? Hiding is quite normal for a cat in a new surrounding and it can sometimes take up to a week before hunger gets the better of them and they venture out. With Bella, hunger was not something she wanted to experience again so it didn't take long for her to find her way to the kitchen where Elise was preparing her dinner. Food was definitely the way to Bella's heart.

As Elise was a writer who spent lots of time at her desk, this was the perfect home for Bella. No noisy children to contend with, no other pets for competition, just the busy tap-tap of the computer as words took form. Bella eventually felt more comfortable and started to abandon her retreat under the sofa. She seemed content to sit near the workstation with the tap-tapping lulling her into a lazy sleep.

At first Elise shut Bella out of the bedroom when it was time for sleep and Bella used this time to explore the whole house, racing up and down the passageway as if some ghostly plague of mice needed to be rounded up and disposed of. Early in the morning, Elise opened the door to allow Bella to come in, then climbed back into bed to see what her reaction would be. Bella would climb up on the end of the bed and watch Elise. She seemed an old soul who didn't normally do things on impulse but watched and waited. With encouragement from Elise, she would edge a little bit closer, ever ready to disappear out the door if she needed to escape. Talking gently, Elise would bring her hand out for her to sniff, then would be allowed to proceed with some gentle scratching around her ears. Bella would purr, something she had learnt to do since she had left her previous sad life behind.

It became routine that Elise would open the door to the bedroom early in the morning and Bella would then make herself cosy on the end of the bed. Progress began when Bella would gingerly walk close to Elise and tap her gently on the arm to make sure she was awake. She was always ready to make an escape but with encouragement from Elise, including lots of ear scratching, escaping seemed to be the last thing on Bella's mind.

After what seemed an age but was in all probability a week, I rang Elise to see how Bella was settling into her new home. While running the rescue I always liked to get updates on how the cat or kitten was progressing and with Bella I was very excited to learn things were going well for her in her new home.

Peninsula Cat Rescue Inc.

December 20, 2014

We are delighted to say that Violet now has a home. This poor little girl suffered so much neglect, lost her babies through starvation, then adopted six hungry little orphans and raised them as her own. After what she has been through she now has a home of her own with a very special lady who rose to the challenge and has formed a bond with her. Watching her transform was one of the most rewarding experiences as a foster carer and no one deserves this more than Violet. She races around her new home as if she can't quite believe it and has even learnt to play. She never goes far from her new owner and likes to sleep on the end of the bed to be near her. She is not a lap cat yet but one thing is certain, she is very happy.

Bella and Elise have been together now several years, and in that time Bella has grown into the most loving, adored companion for Elise. While Elise is busy writing, Bella is just content to be nearby, either in front of the heater on a rug or stretched out by her feet. If Elise goes out into the garden, Bella is by her side, helping to pull weeds, smell the flowers and chase the butterflies.

I'm sure Bella never imagined how luxurious her life would be, coming from such a sad beginning to where she now is. That is the hope for all the cats we rescue, and for Bella being an angry cat is in the distant past.

A Day Out at the Nursing Home

A nurse friend of mine who worked at a Mornington nursing home suggested we take the kittens in to her work so the residents could interact with them. Initially I took the kittens in for a few hours and left them in pens for the residents to come and pat if they wished. There weren't any regular pets there because the policy was that everyone had to agree with having a resident pet and even amongst the elderly in a nursing home there were the pet haters.

After taking the kittens a few times and realising how much the residents were looking forward to their visits, it was agreed my nurse friend would collect them early in the morning and return them in the afternoon after her shift ended. There was a beautiful small courtyard in the middle of the building which had glass all around it. It meant the residents who were wheelchair bound or bed bound could be pushed to the window to observe the kittens playing in the courtyard. We had set up a cat tower, tunnels and toys, and the seat inside the yard was used by the residents to watch their antics or play with them.

Very early in the morning as the sun was rising, I would struggle up the drive in my pyjamas and dressing gown, carrying kittens to be collected. The nurse would then take them to the nursing home and release them into the waiting courtyard.

At first, they were terrified about what may await them, but the confident ones would eventually venture out and start exploring. The residents who were able would then come to the dining room and with great excitement chatter about the kittens. We had to limit the number of residents into the courtyard at a time, but those who loved cats were always nearby in case a kitten looked like it needed a pat. Many of these residents had to give up their pets when they entered the home, which must have been like giving up your children. They were so gentle and loving towards the kittens that I need not have worried about their safety.

If there was a roast or fish for lunch, then the kitchen staff would often save a bit to give to the kittens, and I'm sure there was a bit of ferreting for food off residents' plates going on as well. As a consequence, the kittens would arrive home after their day out totally exhausted, with fat rotund bellies. All they wanted to do was sleep.

At dinnertime when I came to feed them, they would look at their kitten food barely raising an exhausted eyelid and showing total lack of interest. You could almost hear them groan, 'Not more food!'

There was one resident who had been in the home a long

time. She had no known family come to visit her but she had a great love of cats. Every time the kittens came, she would spend time nursing and cuddling them. She would also slip a $50 note into the nurse's hands to help buy food for the kittens. The lady became a palliative care patient who did not have long to live. When it came close to her time to go and she seemed unresponsive, my nurse friend went and collected one of the kittens, then gently placed it on her neck.

Feeling the fur on her skin, she lifted her hand to touch the softly purring kitten and whispered, 'You beautiful little thing.'

Something nice happened to her, and though she had no other family to be with her except the nurses and the kitten, she passed away peacefully.

With tears streaming down their faces, the nurses returned the kitten to its siblings and watched as this bundle of life bounded away.

One day the local press did a story about our visits to the nursing home, and we found a lot more homes for the kittens through the publicity from that article as well as through families who came to visit their relatives. A few kittens also went to the staff members

who loved the visiting guests almost as much as the residents did.

The kittens loved their excursions to the nursing home and they built up confidence each time they went. I would place the cat carrier on the floor with the door open and they would push past each other to get in. When they came to be rehomed, on seeing a carrier open they would automatically go in, thinking they were off to the nursing home.

My nurse friend eventually left her job at the nursing home so the kittens no longer went to visit. I dropped them off a few times after she left, but without her constantly supervising the visiting, I felt it might be too much of a strain on the residents and staff.

Years later I was invited back to give a talk to the residents about the work that we did and I took a few kittens along as examples. I was only minutes into my speech when I realised the residents weren't the least bit interested in what I had to say and all their concentration was centred on the three fluffy guests who were entertaining them. Cutting my talk short I then spent the rest of the time taking the kittens around to be patted and fussed over.

A lady who adopted one of our kittens also worked at another nursing home and invited me along to give a talk and, of course, bring some kittens. It was always best to take some confident, outgoing kittens on these occasions or some smaller ones who were easier to manage.

It was always an exciting time for many residents when the kittens came and the most extraordinary thing to watch was how the dementia patients handled them. They would often nurse a kitten as if it were their own baby and gently sing a lullaby to send it to sleep. There seemed to be some sort of understanding between patient and kitten, with the kitten obliging by nodding off.

Another time, an elderly patient was wheeled in on a bed. She couldn't talk, walk or feed herself, but her face lit up like sunshine dancing on petals when a warm, furry body was placed on her neck. The kitten looked into her eyes, then placed a paw on her chin as if acknowledging the wide smile. I'm sure that patient left the smile on her face for most of the day after her encounter.

Visits to that nursing home had to be limited to the time I could fit in because their courtyard was far too big to let them loose and we would be in danger of losing the kittens.

Another time, I was contacted by a doctor friend of mine to see if we had a suitable cat for a gentleman in a nursing home who would not speak. I knew nothing of the trauma that caused his silence but it was clear he was an unhappy man residing most of the time in his room. He needed something in his life to stimulate him, and he loved cats.

Looking at all the cats we had in our rescue, I settled on one that I thought might be suitable as she was a little shy at first until she got to know you. It might be a project for him to work on, bringing her out of her shell, and it would help him at the same time. My only worry was how she would go with so many other residents to deal with and if it would cause her more stress. The solution was to give it a trial to see how things went, and if it didn't work out, then we would try something else.

I need not have worried as the trial was a big success, except that instead of being a resident cat, she belonged to the man who would not speak. She happily took up residence in the man's room. He fed her, cleaned her litter tray, brushed her and talked to her. Other residents came to admire the cat now happily ensconced on the bed and the conversation with the man revolved around his cat. Our shy little cat was no longer so shy when she had so much attention placed on her and the man who would not talk now had plenty to talk about.

It seemed such a shame when residents had to part with their pets when going into a nursing home. Even some retirement villages are not keen on the residents taking their pets with them into their units with small gardens.

If only we could take the residents to the pounds and shelters to fuss over the inmates, or if only we had more time to take the kittens to the residents. Time was always my enemy and the days could only be stretched so far, but on reflection it seemed such a shame this resource of older residents to help is underutilised. My hope for the future is that this will change.

Poppy

It was close to Christmas when I received an urgent call from another rescue asking if I could possibly squeeze in a mother cat and her newborn babies. The cat had come from a difficult situation and although we were not told of all the circumstances, it was imperative that she be able to raise her babies in safety.

Christmas time in rescue was the worst possible time to receive those phone calls because we were inevitably full, with not a spare place to be found at any of the foster carers.

This situation was urgent as the person asking also worked in a vet clinic and it could have made things very difficult if the clinic became a target for aggression.

The cat and her tiny babies were handed over with the promise that the mother would be returned once the babies were old enough to cope on their own. As we specialised in mother cats with babies and were some distance away, we were contacted to see if we could help.

With some rearrangements a bathroom was made available in our home and a very grateful vet nurse delivered them to us. Knowing only a little of what had happened, I prepared a box for the mum with a towel to be placed over it to give her privacy, fresh food, water and a litter tray.

She was a pretty grey but very thin cat and from experience I guessed she was probably only about 7 months old. When she arrived, she was very quiet, with eyes that seemed distant and resigned. She may have been traumatised so it was important to get her settled as soon as possible. As she and her babies were smothered in fleas, I administered a flea and worm treatment, then placed the towel over the box to make it a cocoon, giving her some privacy.

The following morning on entering the room I discovered she had not eaten anything and the litter tray was unused. Lifting the covering towel off the box, I found the cat lying with her babies attached but with a vacant resigned look on her face. New mothers usually purr when their babies are feeding, but this little cat just lay there robotically doing her duty.

On examining the food that was supplied by the owner, I found it was a cheap dry food with hardly any nutritional value for a nursing cat. If that was all she was used to, I would need to get her accustomed to better food.

Replacing the stale food with fresh, I bent down to gently stroke my new arrival and reassure her that she was safe with us. This somehow seemed to soothe her and she started to relax just a little. While my hand was sliding over her ears in gentle pats, I wondered what this poor little cat had been through. Not knowing many of the particulars of her past was a blessing in a way as my job was to help her raise her babies, along with getting her healthy. Once the fleas and worms had stopped sucking the life from her, she would start to improve, of that I was sure, but she needed food to keep the milk flowing for her babies. So far, she showed no interest in wanting to eat.

With Christmas now passed I offered the mother some leftover turkey to see if it would stimulate her appetite. Warm roast chicken, or in this case turkey, usually had the effect of arousing their interest, but with Poppy, as I now called her, the aroma had little effect.

I tried a can of cat food, placing some on my fingers for her to lick, but again, no response.

Resorting to my next method of appetite stimulant, I placed some kitten wet food in her bowl and managed to get her nose twitching. Perhaps this time she would respond, and having five babies to feed she would surely be getting hungry by now. Placing the food down but within neck stretching distance, I replaced the covering over the box and started to leave the room. Before I reached the door, I heard her eating. Success at last and I had found something she liked, with her devouring it all in one go. I left the room doing a little happy dance.

Premium kitten food is designed to give growing kittens the nutrients they need and after what was possibly a lifetime eating the contents of a cardboard box, Poppy's tastebuds had sprung into action. Her thin body was telling her that this is what it wanted, this is what it liked, and she surrendered to its demands.

Delighting in the success of getting her to eat, I returned to the room with some more kitten food but left it there for her to eat at her leisure. We were making good progress and were on the road to recovery.

The flea treatment had done its job, with dead and dying fleas littering the bedding, leaving red smudgy dots in their wake. It was time to give her some fresh bedding, so carefully placing the baby kittens on a folded towel, I proceeded to remove the old dirty blanket, replacing it with a clean one. Poppy sprang to her feet in panic and tried to hide in the corner, away from her babies and me. Out of the corner of my eye I noticed that there was something not quite right in the way she walked, but at this stage I didn't want to pick her up to examine her. She also seemed to hang her head as if she didn't want to be seen or noticed. I really did wonder what she had been through or seen in her previous life.

Once the babies had been placed back onto the clean bedding, I left the room to fetch her some fresh food and water. On returning I found her nuzzling and cleaning her babies with a look in her eyes that seemed to suggest she approved of the clean surrounds. Pulling the cover back over the box, I left her in peace. I was sure I could hear some faint purring as I left the room. She was feeling safe and secure, it seemed.

Every day, I continued the same routine, with Poppy enjoying the interruption from mothering. Her face would particularly light up when I brought food to her. The kitten food was still in plentiful supply but slowly I added some cooked meat to get her tastebuds used to different foods. She was a willing participant in this trial with her now glossy coat and shiny eyes a testament to its effects.

The kittens were thriving with their now healthy mother doting on them. She no longer tried to hide when I entered the room and the worrying gait she had when she first arrived had disappeared. She was also turning into an attention seeker, bringing her head close to be patted. Through the gentle words of encouragement and telling her what a beautiful girl she was, there were indications of trust. Whatever she had seen or had done to her seemed to be fading as this new life with her babies took over.

The kittens had turned from slug-like bundles of fur to creatures on wobbly legs, and it didn't take long for those legs to start exploring.

The box that had been their home no longer contained them as they scrambled one leg over the other in attempts

to escape. They were confident kittens, now used to being held, stroked and adored. Poppy would watch them with fascination as tentative steps on those wobbly legs gave way to chasing and tumbling. The kittens would soon need to be rehoused in a bigger room with toys and cat scratching trees.

January was always a busy time for us, with many of our kittens being rehomed to families with children on school holidays. Those early days in a new home were crucial in adjusting to their new surrounds, and having family members on hand ensured they had all the attention they needed at this fast-developing stage.

Once the last kitten had been rehomed from the kitten room and sterilisation was administered, Poppy and the babies were moved into their new residence. Instead of hiding as she had when she first arrived, Poppy felt confident in her new room with large windows looking out over the garden. It was very light and airy with several cat scratching trees, toys and boxes for climbing on. These outgoing kittens were in cat heaven, using the equipment to leap upon each other in their games of chase. Poppy often participated in the activities now that she had room to join in. She was still a young cat and possibly didn't have a chance to play in her previous home or was too frightened to make a noise. I never knew.

The fact that I would eventually have to send her back to her previous home invaded my thoughts every now and then, especially now she had filled out and held her head high. Part of the deal in allowing her to come to me was that photos would be supplied to her owner. I dutifully complied, but the dread of handing her back was drifting to the surface and was hard to push away. She was such a sweet little cat with a gentle nature who was growing in confidence every day.

February can be the hottest month in Melbourne and it didn't disappoint. Hot little bodies slept in any cool part of the house, and with so many windows in the kitten room, the heat could become oppressive. It was not unusual on one of these days to find the kittens occupying the dog's bed in the main part of the house with the dog relegated to wherever else she could find. I think the kittens thought that the dog would know the best spots to sleep and much to her annoyance they followed.

Poppy was the perfect guest, and when the door to the kitten room was open, she would never venture far. She would never chase or annoy our cats as other mothers had done in the past. She was so grateful that she was receiving regular good food and her babies were happy. It was hard for me not to get attached to her as I tried to keep a certain distance between us. This strategy failed miserably as she would always come up to me chirping in a musical way for attention, usually resulting in having her ears and chin gently scratched. With her coat in good condition and the extra weight on her she was a very handsome looking cat and given the chance I could have easily found another home for her.

The kittens were now up to the required weight for having their vet work done so arrangements were made. Poppy had to be returned to her owner, so through the third party of the vet nurse who handed her to me, the name and ad-

dress were supplied for the microchip. The owner was happy to pay for Poppy's vet work and the nurse added some extra to help with feeding and care for the past eight weeks. I was so disappointed because if they had reneged on paying for this, there was a good chance they didn't want her back. That was hopeful wishful thinking on my behalf, and the looming dread returned.

Poppy and the kittens recovered quickly from their desexing and the kittens were placed into our adoption program. As they were pretty, outgoing, happy kittens, there was no shortage of new owners wanting them and they were quickly adopted.

Poppy's owners wanted to come and collect her, but I was uncomfortable with this arrangement and replied that she needed a few more days to recover from her operation. She had been a wonderful mother and missed her babies now they had departed, and I wanted to spend some last precious moments with her. She was so calm as I sat with her, stroking her head and under her chin. I wanted to just hug her and say sorry to her over and over. She seemed to sense my melancholy and rested her head on my arm. I was about to betray this trust that we had built up over the weeks I had her with me and it was drilling a hole through my emotional reserves.

My husband agreed to deliver her back to her home and it was with a heavy heart that I brought the cat carrier down to load her in. She struggled at the sight of it and I had to force her in whilst my heart was begging me not to. I closed the door quickly behind her but had to look away. The tears were brimming in my eyes and I didn't want her to see how distressed I was.

Along with instructions on how to feed her properly and supplying sachets to keep her on the food regime she had become accustomed to, I also included a letter. I wanted the owner to understand what a precious little girl they had and what a wonderful mother she had been to her babies. The best I could hope for was to educate them on looking after her properly.

Like a lot of animals, Poppy sensed that something was wrong and tried desperately to get out of her carrier. She kept digging under the blanket I had placed inside, and in failing to escape that way, started pawing desperately at the door, causing a lot of distraction to my husband driving her to her home.

It didn't take long before a strong stench permeated the car. Poppy had loosened her bowels in the carrier, leaving her standing in the sticky smelly substance.

Her beautiful coat had splashes of excrement on it when the car pulled into the driveway. She knew where she was and continued to cry in a pitiful way.

Her owner came out to collect her, with my husband profusely apologising for the mess she was in.

The owner took her inside, and then after a few minutes handed the dirty carrier back. In exchange for the dirty carrier, the letter and food was handed over and my husband continued on his way to work with the offending carrier now in the boot of the car.

On learning of the drama that occurred, my heart remained in a state of dread. I had had no choice but to hand her back and my only hope was that they would now care for her as much as I had.

Over the years I have had so many mother cats and kittens come through our rescue and people often asked if there are any special ones that stick in my mind. This was one case where it didn't have the happy ending I wanted, and my only consolation was that she wouldn't be having any more kittens. I often thought about Poppy and wondered if she was alright. When we rehome cats or kittens, there are never any guarantees that things will work out the way we planned or wanted, but giving one back to a dubious owner was one of the hardest things I have ever done.

Pedigree Cats in Rescue

Over the years working in cat rescue I came across a few pedigree cats that needed rehoming. It always surprised me that an expensive, often very pretty cat would end up with us and many times I didn't know the background of what they had been through.

There was often a different temperament with a pedigree, almost as if they were bewildered that they had ended up in a rescue situation. The cats would look at me as if to say, 'Why am I here? What did I do wrong?' I would look at them and ask the same questions.

It also annoyed me that a pedigree cat would be in such high demand when we advertised them and finding the right home among so many applicants was quite tricky. It made me think how much we are influenced by looks or the perception of an exotic breed. They could have the personality of a cardboard box but if they were pretty to look at, it didn't seem to matter. Sometimes they had an inherent attitude which was easily provoked or was a means of attention seeking.

My first rescued cat, Meggie, was a Scottish Fold who had been abandoned when a boyfriend or partner bought one for his girlfriend, and then the relationship had ended acrimoniously. The kitten was a reminder of the relationship break-up so was left for the next tenant to look after when the owner absconded. This arrangement didn't last long when the authorities came banging on the door and arrests were made. The poor little cat was left outside to fend for herself, and not having any skills as a street cat, went begging to the neighbours for food. Fortunately, one kind lady who had been leaving food out for her put a notice up at the local vet clinic looking for a home for her. We answered the call and she became ours. She was such a pretty-looking cat with no hunting skills whatsoever and obviously thought she belonged on a bed as an adornment.

At the pounds, along with the ordinary kittens coming in there were sometimes cats that looked as though they were a pedigree of some sort. Someone probably thought about backyard breeding their cat, but when it was impregnated by the stray male hanging around and the kittens looked like their dad, they were worthless. If any kittens looked like the pedigree mother, sometimes the kittens were kept for breeding and the mother and ordinary Moggies were left at the pound. There were also times when a Moggie cat had kittens that looked like pedigrees.

We once took in a pregnant black fluffy cat who gave birth to three kittens who could have been Seal Point Ragdolls, and if I hadn't seen it happen with my own eyes, I wouldn't have believed it. We hardly ever showed those kittens because people would fight over the rights to own one and the poor black fluffy mum would be ignored.

All of this pointed to pedigree cats often being seen as a source of making money, and when for differing reasons the idea had been abandoned, they ended up in pounds, shelters or rescue.

Another time, I was contacted about a Burmese cat who was a breeding machine for a backyard breeder. The cat had developed an enormous growth which must have made it very uncomfortable for her to be feeding her babies. This cat had somehow escaped from the premises and became pregnant to a wandering male, resulting in a loss of income from the kittens. The owner of the cat had been persuaded by someone concerned about her health to part with the cat and kittens, and passed the mum to us while keeping the kittens to raise.

On receiving the mother cat, I immediately took her to our vet to assess the growth and her health. She was not in a good way, with the strain of excessive litters taking a toll on her tiny body. On top of that she was having to cope with the engorged growth on her tummy.

It was decided she would be operated on to remove the growth and at the same time she would be desexed. We didn't have long to wait to put her under anaesthetic as there was barely anything in her stomach. That this poor little Burmese cat survived the abuse she received was a testament to her sweet nature. No more babies for her, I promised as she was carried into the operating room.

Some of the vet clinics we worked with in rescue also worked with a lot of cat breeders. Some of them were very supportive of us as a rescue organisation and were very particular about keeping a high standard and their reputation. Others were just a disgrace and should never have been allowed to own cats, let alone breed from them.

One of these breeders contacted me about taking on some of their breeding cats to rehome and would also assist with paying for the vet work that would need to be done. From the conversation it was hard to fathom what was being asked and I somewhat agreed to help, with some conditions attached. I wanted to see the cats in question before making any commitments. The conversation ended with them agreeing to make arrangements for me to visit.

As we were so busy with our normal rescue undertakings, I didn't give another thought to the conversation held with the breeder. If they contacted me, I would deal with it, if not, we had enough work to carry on with.

Many months later I was contacted by someone who had a pedigree cat they wanted help with rehoming. As the cat had been through a horrendous time, they wanted to make sure she went to the best possible home and as a rescue we had a good chance of finding that home for her.

I readily agreed but needed some information to formulate the post to put on our Facebook page and website. What I heard sent shivers down my spine and although I had witnessed many horrific cases of cruelty both at the pound and through my rescue, this case was special and highlights the horrors pedigree cats have to endure.

Tara was 3 years old when rescued, and she had already had four litters of kittens.

The breeders had been reported and an official raid was imminent so the numbers had to be reduced to pass inspection. This is why Tara and her two babies happened to come into the care of Sarah (not her real name).

Tara was one of 24 breeding queens kept in a shed measuring 12 metres by 5 metres. Another shed measuring approximately 5 metres by 5 metres contained the five male cats. The female shed had mesh on one of the doors which let in a little light, but the shed containing the males had no light. There was one couch in the female room which reeked of urine.

The cages were filthy and covered with excrement. There were three feeding bowls filled with dry food which was never enough to feed 24 cats. Those feeding babies often went hungry for days. The water bowls were also in short supply and were often empty. Between all 24 cats there were only four litter trays and they were always overflowing. These mothers were constantly living in their own mess, and for cats, who are obsessive about cleanliness, it must have been sheer hell.

When Tara and her two babies were taken home by Sarah, the first thing she did was give them a bath. The faeces and dirt hidden in their long fur concealed the hundreds of fleas feasting on their tiny bodies, making them anaemic. Tara was a mere 2.5 kg in weight and her 3-month-old kittens were the size of 3-week-old kittens. She didn't care what happened to her anymore; she had no energy left to fight.

Through the lack of nutrition, Tara's teeth had started to decay and her mouth was full of ulcers, leading to her tongue continually hanging out.

After their cleansing bath, Tara and her babies were carefully dried and brushed. They were exhausted from their ablutions so Sarah left them to sleep in their new soft bedding with fresh water and food available nearby. It was touch and go whether they would make it through the night so they were then left alone to minimise their stress.

Both nice and clean ♡♡

The following morning when Sarah went to check on the family, she was happily greeted by Tara, with the babies seeking her attention. They had come through their ordeal and were on the road to recovery.

Sarah wisely allowed the family to go at their own pace in discovering their new abode, and being loved and having small regular meals was just the medicine they needed to build up their strength.

Within a week, one of the kittens became very lethargic and distant. He couldn't be soothed with cuddles, which was very unlike him, so a visit to the vet was arranged.

Upon examination, the vet established that he had a blockage in his bowel and needed immediate surgery. Anxiously awaiting the outcome, Sarah was relieved to hear that he had pulled through and would make a complete recovery. The vet was astounded that this kitten was 3 months old. With his lack of nutrition and not eating enough to keep his organs functioning properly, in addition to anaemia from all the fleas, it was a miracle he had the strength to survive the operation. He was tiny for his age.

The other kitten continued to thrive but there was always an element of hiding back and withdrawing. Both kittens needed to learn social skills and play, something that had been denied them in the breeding sheds they were born in.

Sarah was a trained dog groomer so her skills in handling long fur were useful in keeping Tara and the babies looking their best. Their tiny bodies were starting to fill out with the plentiful food being offered and slowly they were starting to act like normal felines. Tara became so proud of her lovely coat and kept herself and her babies well groomed.

Tara was introduced to the effects of sunshine with daily

outings in the garden. Having only known a dark, rancid shed all her life, she would sit in the sunlight with her head tilted to the sky in homage to the healing rays of the sun. Her groomed coat, now proudly shimmering in the light, would sway in the gentle breeze, a sensation she had never felt before.

The two little kittens started out sitting close to their mother, but gradually, with gentle coaxing from Sarah, they would venture away from their mother's shadow and start to play. Flynn was the more confident of the two, and now that he had healed from his operation would bound up for attention. Coco was more hesitant, but once she saw that Flynn was having fun, decided to take the plunge and join in.

Every day these small steps helped to build their strength and confidence, and now that she was feeling better, Tara started to join in.

Along with the progress in play came the great affection to Sarah and her family. If affection was the only means of showing gratitude for being rescued from their previous life, then Tara and the kittens displayed it in spades. Being Ragdolls, showing affection and commanding attention is in their nature and what they do best. It took Sarah five months to get them back to full strength to be able to have their vet work done.

The kittens easily found loving homes with family relatives but Tara still needed to have work done on her teeth and gums.

Her tongue still hung from her lips, and her mouth needed to recover from the mouth clean because of the ulcers. In time she might also need to have teeth removed as her body was stripped of any calcium-growing nutrients. From her mouth it was hard to guess that she was only 3 years old.

After I posted on our Facebook page the story of Tara, I was immediately inundated with people wanting to adopt her. Having someone who understood her health issues and would be willing to pay for future treatment was an important consideration in selecting the right home for her. As it turned out, someone on acreage, living close to Sarah and with another Ragdoll cat for company, became our first choice for her new home. It meant that Sarah could keep in touch and make sure Tara was settling into her new home.

She was at last having the life she deserved.

It was not usual for me to be directly involved in kitten farm rescue but I had to deal with the consequences a few times. It also explained some of the unusual traits I witnessed when a pedigree cat came through the  rescue. They were just a commodity to some people and, once again, being cats they were disposable.

One day I went to the bank to deposit some funds. One of the tellers there asked if we could assist a cat that was hanging around her place. She and her family had recently moved into a new house along with their own cat and dog.

As soon as they settled in for the night there would be a bloodcurdling howl coming from the front door. On investigation of the source of this noise, they found it was a little Burmese cat wanting to come inside. On opening the door, the cat would bolt into the house, upsetting the dog and family cat who had come to see what the noise was about.

The Burmese cat was gathered up and shown the door, hoping that it would go back to its own home and the new residents could get some sleep.

Every night the same routine happened – howling at the front door elicited exasperated efforts to send the cat back to its own home. Except, this was its home.

On consultation with their new neighbours, they discovered that the little Burmese cat had belonged to the previous owners who had left her behind. Some of the neighbours had fed her after seeing her distressed state but she was getting very thin from lack of food and love.

Whenever I heard the words 'can you help this cat' I would dissolve into a tired resignation that we couldn't really help many cats. By taking them into our homes we upset the dynamic with our own pets and they were not very welcoming to adult intruders. Without having a spare room or enclosure to place them in, it was very difficult to take them on, no matter how desperate the situation. However, after hearing about this poor little Burmese and knowing that a pedigree is fairly easy to rehome, I said I would see what I could do to help her.

As usual at night the Burmese howled at the front door to be let inside and this time she was invited in, but only to be placed in the bathroom. Giving her a bed and some food would make her comfortable for the night, but this little girl, who knew this house so well, wanted everything to be as it used to be. Gone were her family, gone was her bedding and everything familiar. How stressful for a sweet-natured girl who just wanted to be in her home.

After some rearrangement with other foster carers, a room was made ready for my little guest in my home. She was quite chatty and friendly whenever I entered the room and I'm sure she was telling me how outraged she was that her home was not as it should be and her family wasn't in their usual place. I couldn't have agreed more as I tried to soothe her with gentle words and pats. I was sure we would find a loving home for her again.

Some of the neighbours had contacted the previous owners, as they had left their number and address in case any mail was forthcoming for them. They had left the cat behind deliberately and thought that, as she was a nice pedigree cat, the new owners or someone would want her. I'm sure that whatever opinion the neighbours had had of the previous owners changed with this shocking news.

After having a flea treatment and receiving nourishing food, the little Burmese cat started to lose her indignation at being left behind and soon settled into her room. She was very skinny still and quite exhausted from trying to survive outside. She needed lots of rest and gentle words, something I was more than happy to give her. It was so rewarding to see her eyes light up whenever I entered the room with her food. She would soon forget the past and I would make sure she had a better home to go to.

After a few weeks of care, it was time to advertise for a new home for our pedigree cat. She was delightful but did have a few quirks in her nature that the new owner would need to be aware of.

As usual after our Facebook post, it was apparent a lot of people were wanting to own a pedigree cat and I had no shortage of people wanting to take her in. We settled on a lovely couple who had another Burmese and wanted a companion for her. After several phone calls to enquire that all was going well, the little cat settled in, taking command of the bed in the master bedroom. She was back in her rightful place, being loved and adored again.

With so much emphasis placed on puppy farms and the horrendous conditions some of those breeding animals are placed in, spare a thought also for the poor pedigree cats who sometimes endure worse conditions. They are also shut away in sheds, like Tara, or tucked away in homes where no one can see them, just another commodity. If you are ever in a position to get a pedigree, make sure you do your homework and check to make sure you are not encouraging further appalling breeding establishments.

My grateful thanks to Sarah and others like her who bravely take a stand and try to make a difference to kitten farms and puppy farms. Tara and her kittens escaped, but many more don't and this is the sort of life they endure.

Cats in Welfare

It was while working as a volunteer in the pound that I came across community service workers, people who had committed a crime and whose sentence was doing community service to pay penance for their crime. The people I worked alongside were mostly young people who loved animals and were very keen to help with cleaning, feeding or whatever duties were asked of them to count as their community service.

Sometimes I was also asked if I would rehome a cat belonging to someone who was sentenced to jail. The cat had to be surrendered to the pound by the owner doing time. Most of the cats I rehomed were lovely and had obviously been taken care of by their previous owner. Many a time I heard the saying that the person hated humans but loved animals and I felt privileged that I was entrusted with probably the most precious thing they treasured, which was their pet. I learnt from those early years not to make judgements.

Over the years, while running the rescue, I would be contacted by someone wanting help with kittens they had that they wanted to make sure went to good homes. Upon going to collect these kittens, I would be astounded at the properties I was invited to, and I'm sure even the police would hesitate to go to some of them. Because I cared about the animals and didn't stand in judgement, I was trusted to come and collect them.

I would make arrangements with my deputy that if I hadn't resurfaced in half an hour, to call the police. Always when I returned to my car with the kittens safely in the carrier I would ring to say I was alright and no need to alert the authorities. Because I was never in a uniform, I was permitted to enter a property and quite often the inhabitants would be quite chatty about their love for their pets. I would listen intently and offer advice and help if needed. Once again I was careful to never pass judgement but would gently educate them about ways they could improve the health and welfare of their pets. Mostly I had to reassure them that I would take good care of their kittens and find them the best homes.

Except for needing flea and worm treatment, they were usually in very good health and very friendly.

My vet sometimes referred the occasional welfare case to me to give them help with a pregnant cat or kittens. One lady lived in a notorious building and I had some reservations about entering it. Meeting me at the gate, the lady escorted me through the maze of residents watching us climb to her tiny unit at the top of the building, where a heavily pregnant cat kept her company. The cat had belonged to the next-door neighbours who had vacated the premises, leaving her behind. The lady was concerned about how fat the cat had become and was incredulous when told that perhaps the extra fat she was carrying contained babies.

Leaving the lady with extra food to build up the expectant cat, I arranged for her to notify me once the babies were born and I would give her guidance on looking after the mum while she raised her babies.

In the early stages all was going well and once again I climbed the stairs to her apartment with lots of suspicious eyes focused on me. As this building had a reputation, I'm sure there were cameras all around and no doubt the police were also wondering what I was doing in that area. With encouragement, the lady raised the kittens until they became too difficult for her to handle, and at about 6 weeks of age I decided to take the boisterous kittens home. Arrangements were also made for her to have the mother desexed and for her to remain as the lady's companion. She was a sweet little cat who no doubt cherished having an owner who cared for her after the last ones gave her up. As for the lady, she had someone who loved her unconditionally even in her difficult living arrangements. There was a possibility that she might be moved to a better place to live and I hoped she and her cat would be given that chance.

One day a call came from a building supplies shop explaining they had caught a small kitten in their yard and asked if I would take it into the rescue. With all the forklifts racing around and the clatter of timber being loaded it was no wonder this little kitten was terrified.

One of the staff members had managed to throw a coat over it and brought it to the staff bathroom in readiness for my arrival. Taking a look at the kitten spitting and shaking in the corner, I decided my thick gloves would be needed to transfer it into the waiting carrier.

When I arrived home, I put my little capture, still in the carrier, into a cupboard under the stairs until I decided where best to place it. The kitten would need working on to bring it around, and having a quiet, dark, cocoon-like space might be the best place to make a start.

It only took a matter of days for the little kitten to come out for food and to start to use the litter tray, and although still very shy, she was definitely a fast learner.

It was time for her to learn social skills so the carrier, as well as her tray, was moved into the kitten room along with other kittens of a similar age. The carrier was her safety place if it was all too overwhelming for her, but thankfully that didn't last long. The other kittens would come over and poke their heads in to see what was inside, and before long she became one of the gang and the carrier was removed.

It was fascinating watching this little kitten develop. She would observe as the other kittens chased each other, tumbling over each other in their games of chase. It was almost as if she had formed the words 'Is that what I'm meant to do?' and then, after a few hesitant starts, she would join in the fun. Kittens being kittens, playtime soon dissolved into naptime and with their energy sapped, they would all curl up together with limbs and paws sprawled over each other like an octopus. In the middle of all this was my little store kitten.

A phone call came from a lady wanting a kitten for her young daughter. I vaguely knew this lady and when she arrived with her daughter I learnt the distressing story of why they wanted a kitten.

Her husband had turned violent one night during an argument with his wife and the child had witnessed the incident. It was a domestic violence case where the perpetrator had continually worn down the victim until she bravely decided she had to get away.

Arriving at the police station with a compassionate friend, the lady told her story of continual threats of violence against her and her children and through her tears said that this shouldn't happen to someone like her. She was intelligent, beautiful, had a good job, a fabulous house and two beautiful children, yet she was a victim of domestic violence.

There are no lines defining who will be affected by domestic violence. It can happen to the rich, the poor and all those variations in between.

The lady had managed to rent another house nearby and with supporting friends managed to get a semblance of her life together again. After viewing her father in a fit of rage, the little girl had lost her voice and chose not to speak. After several visits to a child psychologist, it was suggested the child might like a pet, like a kitten or a puppy. Most of her toys and familiar things were taken away from her, so having something of her own to care for might help with regaining her lost voice.

The day they came to view the kittens, they were in a playful mood and happily bounded up for pats. All except the shy little kitten from the building store. She hung back and observed as she usually did until she felt it was safe to take part in the activities the others were involved in.

The girl was given the choice of any kitten to take and surprisingly she pointed her finger at the shy kitten who held back. I looked at the mother with raised eyebrows and wondered if the shy kitten would be suitable. Wouldn't an outgoing, super-friendly one be more appropriate?

With concern, the mother again asked her daughter which kitten she wanted, and again the finger pointed to the shy kitten.

Usually, I would ring about a week later to see how the kitten was settling in, but this time the mother beat me to it. 'Snuggles', as she was named, was doing particularly well, and best of all, her daughter was talking again. Snuggles was taken to bed at night and under the blankets the little girl would talk to her and tell her not to be frightened and that she would look after her.

Every night Snuggles would curl up close and the two would be intertwined as if they were siblings. They had formed a special bond and both would grow up together, being there for each other. Snuggles had broken the pain barrier.

Running a rescue meant I received a lot of phone calls and one stood out for me. A man phoned wanting a cat for a companion, and after asking a lot of questions I was still uncertain whether he was a suitable applicant for one of our kittens or cats. He seemed to slur his words slightly, or it may have been a bad phone connection, but I wanted to be sure. He had all the right answers to my questions and he seemed to be coherent but I was still unsure. As we were attending a pet store for meet and greets, I arranged for him to meet me there.

While we were setting up, one of the staff members came over and mentioned a man had been waiting for us to arrive and wanted to speak to me.

After settling the kittens and cats into their pens, I went to speak to him, soon realising it was the man I had arranged to meet.

My initial reservations dissolved when I heard his story. He worked on nightshift and had waited up until I arrived, which accounted for his slightly slurred speech. He wasn't a confident man but he was also very tired and waiting for me cut deeply into his sleep time.

He had been in a relationship where there were two adored cats, and as the relationship had ended with the cats going to his partner, he was lonely.

He had set himself up in rented accommodation and supplied a letter from his landlord allowing him to have a cat, but there was one stipulation, he wanted a cat that would watch movies with him.

That was an unusual request and one I hadn't come across before, so I had to think hard on who would be a suitable companion to watch movies with. Most of our kittens were fairly boisterous and needed someone to entertain them a lot of the time or they would be asleep. None of our mother cats were available but I did have an older kitten, about 8 months old, who was very shy. My husband had been picking her up and placing her on his chest as he read in bed, and although she started out too terrified to move, she had begun to accept it.

She was slowly adjusting to being held but I wondered if it was too soon to rehome her, and whether someone who was away all night but home during the day would be suitable. She may do the opposite of sleeping on the bed and watching movies with him and instead hide away.

As the man was used to cats from his previous relationship, he wanted to give it a try and see if he could continue to bring her out of her shell. If it failed, she would come back to us and we would continue to work on her. I gave him a week's trial to see how she went, fully expecting her to be returned to us.

After a few days I thought about contacting the man to see if there was any bonding going on between them, but my impatience had to be curtailed to give them a chance to get to know each other. I had to give them time.

The week went by, and unable to contain my concern any longer, I called the man, expecting to hear disappointment.

'I'm afraid I have some bad news for you,' he said in a stern voice. 'I won't be returning your cat. She is just perfect!'

Not quite believing what I was hearing, I was desperate for more information.

It appeared the cat loved watching movies, starting off by sitting on the couch next to him, and then gradually moving onto his lap for pats and ear scratches. She was that little bit older and nothing was known of her past, but it turned out she loved being the centre of attention when he came home from work, yet she didn't mind if she was left on her own for hours. He was besotted.

The next time I was in the store, there was a voucher waiting for me to use for our cat rescue. Also, the man had practically bought the store out with a new bed, toys, cat scratching posts, and everything a cat desired. She was one very spoilt cat and was getting the best that money could buy.

On phoning the man to thank him for the voucher, I could hear the sheer pleasure he was getting from his companion as they watched movies together.

'You have made a lonely man very happy, thank you.'

Finding a great loving home for a shy cat is one of the best feelings you could ever have and made all our work worthwhile.

Another phone call that stood out for me was a short message from a woman saying she didn't have much credit on her phone and could I call her back please.

I thought about my own rather large phone bill, but there was something about the voice that made me want to ring her back straightaway.

The lady said she had a near new cat scratching tree she wanted to donate to us as she no longer had room for it.

I was often taking on new foster carers and we tried to outfit them with enough equipment to make their life easier. A near new cat scratching tree was always welcomed for little kittens to use.

Arrangements were made to meet the lady at a storage facility, and after the initial introductions and making sure she didn't want to keep the cat tree, I learnt about her life.

This lovely lady was made homeless as so many others like her. She had divorced her husband and had become homeless through no fault of her own. She had been sleeping in her car with her cat, moving along the coast where there were toilet facilities for washing herself. She had been fortunate in that a small two-bedroom unit had been assigned to her, so along with her cat she was able to have her disabled daughter come and live with her. As well as the new home, the lady had found a part-time job, which gave her enough money to keep her car going and pay vet bills as they arose. The problem was that the cat scratching tree took up so much room that there wasn't any space left for other things, which were now sitting in the storage unit. The cat would have to make do with the bed or a snuggle on a lap, something I'm sure the cat didn't mind.

While loading the cat scratching tree into my car, the lady asked if I knew anyone needing a lawnmower. She particularly wanted it to go to someone in need as she no longer had any use for it. I couldn't think of anyone off the top of my head but what she said really started to affect me. This lovely, kind lady was thinking of someone who might be worse off than her and had a need for a lawnmower. She could have easily advertised it for sale and made a bit of money to pay a bill or treat herself.

She was one of many who probably worked before getting married but had been the main caregiver. She probably kissed her children goodbye at the school gate, before going home to make her house neat and tidy. She probably baked goods or made items for fundraising in the school or sporting club. She was like any one of us, but she belonged to the generation where women were less educated and were paid less than men for the same work, with no superannuation for retirement. And if she divorced, or sometimes was left widowed, she didn't have enough capital to buy another home. She was part of the fastest growing statistic of homelessness in Australia, and there but for the grace of God went any one of us. What a shabby way to treat older women.

On delivering the cat tree to my foster carer, I regaled her with the story and asked if she knew of anyone in need of a lawnmower.

As it happened, my foster carer needed one and although they had a ride-on mower for the large lawns, they needed a smaller one for the lawn around the house. But she was insistent that they pay for it, even if the lady just used the money for her cat's needs. The exchange did take place, with my foster carer giving her a little extra to help with her cat vet fees.

Over the years I have been asked to take on kittens and cats from various welfare cases and not all of them ended happily. Sometimes it was from damaged people who damaged their animals. Sometimes it was children who indulged in cruelty with no empathy for the animal, taught by uncaring parents.

An unusual request came one day to find a home for a cat from an unlikely source. A vet had taken possession of a lovely cat that was surrendered to him and he wanted some help with rehoming it.

The cat had belonged to a wealthy family who were going overseas to spend several months at their other home, and as they were unable to take the cat with them and no one was going to be home to look after it, they wanted it euthanised. They were not interested in placing it in boarding kennels for the time they were away and so the decision was made to put the cat down. If the children wanted another cat, then they would get a kitten when they returned.

Horrified that anyone could be so blasé about their pet, the vet contacted me for help and I readily agreed.

The vet ended up finding a lovely home for the unsuspecting cat but it made me wonder what sort of morals and values these parents were teaching their children.

In this case I did stand in judgement and there were a few others that were similar which made me realise that having a flash house or car doesn't always translate into the best home for a pet.

Oliver's Army

A call had come from the local pound about an 8-week-old kitten who had been hit by a car resulting in his jaw being out of alignment, and would we be prepared to take him on. Knowing that without our help the kitten stood little chance of living, I agreed to bring him into our rescue.

On collecting him from the pound it was obvious this

little boy needed some major work and although the pound vet had given him painkillers, I made an appointment with our own vet for a further assessment.

After examining him, the vet found that the kitten's jaw had been pushed to one side by the impact, which meant a specialist vet would need to operate to try and correct it so that he could live some sort of normal life. Our vet thought the cost would run into thousands of dollars, something our little rescue could ill afford, especially with kitten season in full swing and so many mouths to feed.

Our vet rang the specialist clinic on our behalf to get some sort of estimate on the cost and put the case forward for a discount if it could be arranged. After prescribing some more painkillers, an appointment was made with the specialist clinic to see our newly arrived little kitten.

The other problem I had was finding a foster carer experienced enough to care for the kitten through his recovery. This was quickly solved by one of my carers wanting to take on the challenge. As she had been a practising doctor in South Africa but was not currently working, she volunteered to take on caring for and raising the kitten.

Oliver, as we named him, was a very endearing grey, fluffy kitten who seemed to know we were doing our best to make him better. Even through his pain he would purr loudly and look adoringly into your eyes, making everyone who met him melt with love. We all wanted him to get through this traumatic ordeal, but how were we going to pay for his operation on our meagre budget? We had already paid several hundred dollars on medicines and consultations, so how would we be able to afford the operation and the special food he needed?

I decided to go public on our Facebook page and see if there was someone who would be willing to take him on.

1 February 2014

PCR has recently taken in an 8-week-old kitten who was clipped by a car, causing his jaw to be broken. Oliver was given painkillers, but to realign his jaw will cost $1500 with a specialist vet.

We are not in a position to outlay this amount so his prognosis is not promising. Oliver was placed into foster care to see how he would manage with eating and drinking, and this gutsy little boy has exceeded all our expectations. Not only is he eating soft food, but also he is attempting to clean himself afterwards. Except for his jaw being out of alignment, he is a normal playful, very affectionate kitten and we would like to do our best to give him a normal life.

As we have many other healthy normal kittens also needing homes, we would like to offer Oliver up to someone who has the means to have his jaw fixed and to give him a loving home. The operation needs to be done as soon as possible as he is still a growing boy.

If you are in a position to give this dear little boy the operation he needs or would like to help in any way, please contact us

I had barely finished the post when suddenly the comments came rolling in with a gentleman saying he would offer us $50 to get the ball rolling on a fund for Oliver. Others also began to make us offers, so we quickly gave out our banking details and organised a PayPal account. The donations were to be marked 'Oliver' and Oliver's Army of helpers was born.

Within 24 hours we had raised $2420, enough to cover our vet bills, the operation and food for Oliver. We were astounded. We couldn't believe how generous people had been, and to top it off, we had someone who wanted to adopt him. Jaimie and her family had seen the photos of Oliver, and along with making a generous donation, wanted to adopt him.

Working in rescue came with a cavalcade of emotions, sometimes very low and sometimes very high. This result pushed our emotions through the stratosphere.

Oliver had a doctor as a foster carer, a specialist vet who thought he was rather special, and a new owner. It didn't get much better than that.

I wrote another Facebook post to Oliver's Army of helpers.

3 February 2014

With your help Oliver is now booked in for his operation on Wednesday morning. We are all so grateful that you have given him this opportunity of living a normal life. Thank you from all of us at PCR.

After placing Oliver in a carrier lined with lots of soft padding, I made the journey to the specialist vet for his operation.

To keep his supporters informed I posted again on our Facebook page.

5 February 2014

Latest update on Oliver is that a piece of his jaw is missing, so instead of a plate being inserted, he has to have an external fixation which will wire his jaw back. It can be removed in 4–6 weeks if the mouth has realigned. There was substantial damage, including a very swollen tongue which is of the most concern at the moment. He will need monitoring overnight and will be released back to us in the morning if all goes well. He is such a brave little boy.

We were all so relieved when told the operation was successful, but he did have a contraption fitted to his jaw that would make eating quite a chore. He would have to be cleaned after each meal, and because he was a hungry boy who had no respect for contraptions barring his way, it became quite messy.

We also learnt later that the specialist vet who had operated on Oliver developed a soft spot for him and also offered to give him a home if one was needed.

6 February 2014

We brought Oliver home from the vet and were told he charmed everyone, including the surgeons.

This brave little boy had to pass the eating test and not only did he pass but they had to stop him eating in case he burst. He has such a zest for life so it will be challenging for him to be wrapped in cotton wool for several weeks. Starting with his Elizabethan collar, which he was not impressed with.

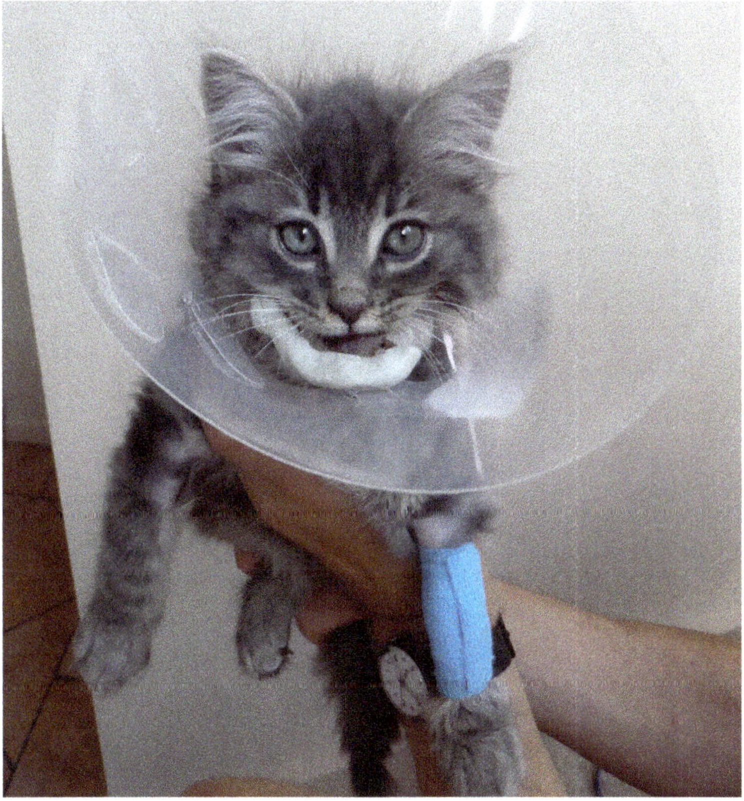

Our foster carer tirelessly worked on feeding and cleaning Oliver, but it was decided that for him to bond with his new owner, it would be best if she took over caring for him.

8 February 2014

Oliver is going to be handed over to his new owner for nursing and bonding. He has to have his collar removed so he can eat and Ollie likes to eat as if it is his last meal. This means his external fixture gets smothered in food so he needs to be regularly wiped down and kept clean.

He is a little frustrated at not being able to run around with the other kittens, so we feel he will bond with his new family and will hopefully lead a quieter life while he recuperates. He needs regular check-ups over the next few weeks and adjustments as needed, so we will keep you informed on his progress. Thank you again for allowing this charming boy, who has stolen all our hearts, a chance of a normal life.

Oliver would no doubt thank you all himself but his preoccupation at the moment is how to get this contraption off so he can eat faster.

With sadness and happiness intertwined, Oliver was handed over to Jaimie to look after. Our foster carer had loved every minute of caring for him, but with instructions now passed on, we said a sad farewell to our little boy.

True to her word, Jaimie kept us informed on how Oliver was progressing, which we then passed on to Oliver's Army.

11 February 2014

Hi Joy and to everyone that has fallen for my gorgeous boy Oliver.

I thought I would give you all an update on how this tough little boy is going. Oliver has made himself right at home and is certainly making it known to my other two cats and Staffy dog who rules the roost. This little ball of fluff had them all running scared.

It has been an enormous learning curve helping him to eat each meal and then the clean up afterwards – cause he gets food everywhere. Ears, face, chest, feet. I wonder if anything is actually being swallowed.

Bath time is our special time. He is quite happy to be wrapped in a towel and cuddled whilst I clean all the food off with baby wipes and cotton buds. It is so traumatic for him that the only way he can deal with it is by sleeping with his massive engine running.

Despite the collar, he happily plays, explores and climbs like any normal kitten should. It has been quite a task to limit his activity to prevent any damage to his jaw.

He had a check-up at the vet today and they are extremely happy the external fixture is stable and clean. He has to go back to the surgeon on Thursday, however, so they can assess his jaw. Unfortunately, due to the extensive damage, it hasn't quite aligned properly so he will have to have his jaw re-broken to sort this out. They think this will occur once the bones heal. It was really hard to hear, I must admit. My first thought was 'Hasn't this boy been through enough?' but I know that he will take it in his stride and I am looking forward to the many years of love and fun we will have once we get through these next few months.

I just wanted to say THANK YOU to each and every one that kindly donated to give this little boy a second chance, and to Peninsula Cat Rescue, keep up the amazing work. I will keep you all posted on Oliver's progress because I know he worked his way into all your hearts just like he did mine. Jaimie.

Jaimie took Oliver into work with her each day so that he could be fed and cleaned for the 4–5 times a day ritual. Oliver took it all in his stride and as the morning sun streamed into her office, he would settle comfortably with Chilli the dog and soak up the sun's rays.

Two months later Jaimie again updated us on Oliver's progress, so naturally I posted again to Oliver's Army of helpers.

16 April 2014

Just an update on Oliver (or Ollie as he is affectionately known). Since we last spoke he has had his jaw brace and head collar removed. He has been desexed and microchipped and is eating kitten food by the bucketload. His jaw has continued to straighten as he has grown and there is no sign of tenderness which means there will be no further operations at this stage. He is a big smoocher and loves to hop into bed with us on a nightly basis. I want to thank everyone for giving this beautiful boy a second chance.

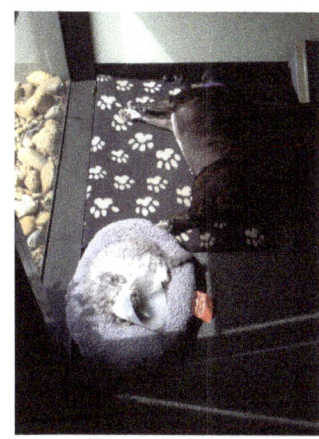

Being a regular passenger in the car going to and from work meant that Ollie loved going for car rides. He would often be a spectator when Jaimie's son went to footy practice and would sit on the dashboard or back seat waiting for them to return.

The love of the car continued and Ollie, living on a farm, would regularly run up the long driveway and greet them when they came home. He loved to hop in the car and hang out the window like a dog as they drove the rest of the way to the house.

As Jaimie said, 'Little did I know when I adopted that cute ball of fluff how much love, laughter and antics he would bring to our family. He has the most personality of any cat I have ever known and we couldn't imagine our family without him.'

LETTERS FROM A LITTLE BLACK CAT

JOY HERRING

Bonnie and Matilda

A phone call from a wildlife carer came one morning asking if I had room for a heavily pregnant cat. The wildlife carers were some of many volunteers who go out at night looking along roadsides for any wildlife that may still be alive after being hit by a vehicle. In this case it was a major highway with only a few entry and exit points, encased by high fencing or walls. In the torchlight near a drain was an indistinct bundle of white fur, possibly a possum or other small mammal. On closer inspection they found a very heavily pregnant cat, almost too weak to stand on her own.

Carefully wrapping her up in a towel, taking care in case she was feral and about to lash out, they carried her to their car and placed her gently in a carrier. The cat was too weak to do anything other than surrender to their care. They then took her home to assess their find.

Placing the carrier in a bathroom, they were able to get a good look at the cat. Being wildlife carers, they didn't have any cat food so a little of their dog's food was substituted, along with any other meat from the fridge they thought would tempt her. It was patently obvious that this was a friendly cat who had been someone's pet and somehow had ended up in the ditch on a busy highway.

With gratefulness in her eyes, she hungrily devoured the food on offer before collapsing into a deep sleep on the towels.

In the morning, the wildlife carers rang around to see if anyone was able to take the cat and as most rescues were full, my name was suggested as someone who might be able to take her.

I had a bathroom I could make available, so one of the carers drove her to me. While settling her into her new lodgings in the bathroom, I heard from the carer how surprised they had been to have a cat in their possession instead of the usual wildlife victim. As it was a fairly busy, well-used highway, I thought it likely that she had been pushed out of a car to fend for herself. I had seen and heard it so often that nothing surprised me, but guessing what happened to her took a back seat to the reality of getting her well. Even though she was terribly thin, I guessed from her rotund belly that it wouldn't be long before she gave birth. I had to get her up to strength as quickly as I could to cope with the imminent arrival and feeding of her babies.

The first thing needing attention was the mass of fleas covering her body, so after ascertaining from the vet that it was safe to do so, I then flea and worm treated her.

Having a safe and comfortable room to herself, my new guest's face would light up whenever I entered her room. With dead and dying fleas covering her blanket with brown blotches, she would patiently wait while I exchanged a dirty covering for a fresh one. She was more steady on her feet now, with the nourishment of the food giving her strength.

Settling down in the fresh bedding, this dear little cat would then put her paw out to touch me as if thanking me for taking care of her. It was at that moment that a special bond grew between us and I was determined that I would do everything I could to make up for the horrible past she must have endured. The name Bonnie sprang into my head and seemed to suit her so well.

I then placed a post on our Facebook page to inform people of our new arrival.

10 February 2015

It is hard to comprehend how a beautiful little cat like Bonnie is treated with so little thought for her welfare. She was found heavily pregnant and in a ditch beside a major highway, starving and unable to move any further. She has a wound on her neck either from an attack or from a blunt object. Since she has been with us, this dear little girl has not stopped purring and she knows she and her babies will be safe as the birth cannot be far away. The tragedy is that there are so many out there like Bonnie, discarded, wounded, starving, bewildered and wondering what they did wrong to be so easily discarded by their human carers.

With a full tummy, maternity ward at the ready and lots of pats and words of encouragement, Bonnie is one of the lucky ones and she certainly knows it. Just like so many of our other mother cats.

Bonnie was still very weak from her ordeal, but to make matters worse, the flea and worming treatment was starting to take effect. Along with dead and dying fleas came the diarrhoea and vomiting. She seemed to be embarrassed by my having to clean the litter tray so often or clear up bits of vomit, but my reassurance to her that she would be alright and gentle stroking was rewarded with the paw coming out to touch me. It really was a race against time to get her well before her babies arrived.

Once again I posted on our Facebook page the update on Bonnie.

17 February 2015

Update on Bonnie who was found in a ditch beside a major highway. Since being flea and worm treated, life has not been easy for this lady in waiting. She was starving when found so we had to regulate how much food she should have. On top of this she was riddled with fleas and no doubt worms as well so it has taken a toll on her young body with vomiting and diarrhoea. We are hoping that she can regain her strength before the babies arrive or we run the real danger of her rejecting them. Quite often we hear people say they want their pet to experience motherhood as an excuse not to get them desexed. The reality is that cats like Bonnie do not have the strength or will to be mothers. It is thrust upon them often by people putting human emotions onto a cat.

After a few days, the worms were not so visible but the diarrhoea continued. Bonnie was already in a weakened state from hunger, but once the main source of worms left, her appetite returned and she devoured all the food I placed in front of her. To start with, I gave her small meals with some cooked chicken, along with the high energy food recommended by the vet. Her eyes were certainly brighter and her coat, which was dull when she first came, started to take on a healthier sheen. Not having so many parasites feeding off her made such a difference and the babies would now be receiving some much-needed nourishment in the womb.

Along with the appetising food, Bonnie also needed a lot of sleep as part of her recovery.

It wasn't long before I heard her start to meow loudly. I quickly went into her room and it was clear she was in labour. My excitement was tinged with anxiety about whether she would be strong enough to cope with the birth. Once again, she held out her paw to me to hold while the contractions grew stronger. As I gave her gentle words of encouragement, the first little bundle arrived and like all mothers she began licking to stimulate breathing. Mother nature now took over and my role as encourager took a back seat while the obligatory cleaning process was progressing in earnest. The loud purring by Bonnie encouraged the new arrival to search for a teat and before long it had latched on to the life-giving nipple.

It was hard to tell from all the licking and nuzzling for a teat what the new arrival's colour was, but from a distance it appeared to have similar shades as Bonnie.

Taking a rest from all the ablutions, she looked at me with pride in her eyes. She was now a mother.

Once again, the paw came out for me to hold while another contraction shook her body. The gratefulness this little cat was showing me by allowing me to hold her paw in this intimate moment was such a powerful message of love. To see that she had absolute trust in me after being abandoned by her previous owners was overwhelming and tears sprang to my eyes when I reflected on it.

Once more another furry bundle arrived, but this time

there was no confusion in the routine. She knew what to do and the new baby knew it had to find a teat to suckle. I was having a lesson on the wonder of nature and Bonnie wanted me to be part of it.

Another three babies arrived soon after, with Bonnie holding out her paw with the contractions. Each baby looked similar to the previous ones.

She was the picture of pure contentment with her five babies suckling on her teats. She was exhausted from the delivery but knew she was safe and being cared for.

As a courtesy to the wildlife carer who had rescued Bonnie from the ditch, I rang to express my gratitude for rescuing her and to tell her the good news of the safe arrival of the babies. This news was received with great happiness, and although many wildlife carers have issues with roaming cats, I have met many who care about them and realise that many cats are dumped or abandoned without any thought to their survival.

During my time in rescue, I was often called by wildlife carers to take on abandoned kittens found in the bush and sometimes these carers adopted one of the kittens for their own family. Our job in rescue was to raise them in the family home and have them socialised with other cats, dogs and children. Included in our work was raising awareness of the harm cats could do to wildlife and encouraging new owners to either keep them inside or to build a cat enclosure, to keep them from harm as well as away from wildlife.

After my children had vacated the family home, I had some helpers come to socialise and play with the kittens. One of these assistants was a university student called Lucy who came to help in between lectures and assignments. Lucy's job was to spend time playing with the kittens, paying particular attention to any shy ones that might need a bit more encouragement.

Lucy had watched the bond grow between Bonnie and myself and saw how the paw came out to greet me every time I went in the room. She was such a special cat with big eyes that seemed to gaze right into your soul. Lucy knew someone who might be the perfect match for Bonnie, once her babies were old enough for her to leave. I listened with hope as she described the person who had recently retired and was on her own. She had grown up with cats but had never owned one herself and the family thought she needed a reason to get up each day. Having a mother cat find a home before her babies was rare but I remained hopeful that this could be that someone special for Bonnie.

Bonnie's diarrhoea had cleared up and her health continued to improve. She loved receiving food regularly and her babies were thriving. Her happiness in her situation was borne out by the loving look in her eyes and the constant raising of her paw to be taken by my hand. I was going to find it very difficult to part with this cat who had found her way into my heart.

Many people asked me how I could part with the kittens I raised or rescued. If they were going to a loving home it wasn't all that difficult, but I had great trouble parting with the mothers. Being a mother myself, I could imagine how it would feel to be abandoned in my hour of need, trying to raise babies the best way I could. We become empathetic to a mother cat and a special bond forms between us.

It was during this time that I received a phone call from Mallee Cats Rescue, a rural rescue group I sometimes worked with, to see if I could take on another mother cat with her baby that had been left behind when the previous owners of a farm moved out. They had left her without any food or water and two of her three babies had already died. The new owners didn't want her or the responsibility of looking after her or her baby, so arrangements were made to bring her down to me.

Another mother cat and her baby shouldn't be too much trouble so a room was made ready for their arrival.

Once again, the mother was very skinny but the baby, about 5 weeks old, appeared healthy, though a little bit timid. I don't know the background of a lot of our new guests but I could see this cat was melancholic and sad. She seemed very depressed and there was no life in her eyes, just resignation to her fate. How anyone could do this to their pet always astounded me, but dealing with reality meant I didn't have the luxury of dwelling on it.

Matilda, as I named my new arrival, needed building up and her little kitten needed to build up trust.

Whenever there were new arrivals into the rescue, I always put up a Facebook post describing a little about them so that people could follow their journey, and hopefully it would also lead to a new beginning in a loving home.

10 March 2015

I wonder if people who abandon their cats when they leave their house ever think about the consequences of their actions. Take Matilda and her babies who were only found when the new owner took possession of the house and found them in residence. There she was, practically starving and trying to nurse three little babies. She is rescued, losing two babies, then comes to us where she has plenty of food and comfort. But Matilda seems depressed, melancholic and sad. She never purrs, but is now

feeding and nursing her baby again. I think when her owners left her behind, they left her with a broken heart.

Today, after lots of kind words and patting, there was a breakthrough. Matilda started to purr.

I now had two mother cats with babies to care for, one who held her paw out to touch me during labour and the other needing to learn to trust a human again.

Lucy was set with the task of talking gently to Matilda and teaching her kitten how to play. Starting off slowly, the kitten became inquisitive and was soon chasing after the toys but never ventured far from her mother's watchful gaze.

Matilda was steadily gaining weight and with it came a glossy sheen on her coat and a shine in her eyes. She was starting to purr whenever Lucy or I came into the room, especially if it involved food. I don't think cats ever forget the time when they were starving because feed time was always the highlight of the day. Both Bonnie and Matilda would ravenously gulp their food down as if it were their last meal. It was a trait of many mother cats I rescued.

Bonnie and her babies were all thriving and my reward for caring for them progressed from a paw in the hand to a full-blown cat hug. She would nestle her head under my chin when being held and wrap her paws around my neck, while her body shook from the purring vibrations.

I was so in love with this cat. How on earth was I going to betray her by passing her on to someone else. Who would be good enough for this poor darling who had been through so much? While luxuriating in the intimacy of this embrace, I put all thoughts of rehoming to the back of my mind. It didn't bear thinking about and I would worry about it closer to the time.

Lucy regularly came to help with the kittens and had made a lot of progress with Matilda and her baby. Bonnie's babies were turning into little rascals, running and chasing after each other in the bathroom. They needed more room to run around and Bonnie, doting mother that she was, needed some space away from them.

While watching the kittens at play, I mentioned to Lucy how hard it was going to be to part with Bonnie when the kittens had gone to their forever homes. Lucy had been discussing with her family the possibility of Marilyn, a relative, giving Bonnie a home. They thought that being at home after retirement would be lonely so the prospect of taking on Bonnie was suggested to her. Marilyn wasn't sure this was what she wanted so a meet and greet was arranged for her to visit Bonnie.

Bonnie and her kittens were sleeping when Marilyn arrived with Lucy and her mother. As usual, her face lit up when I entered the room but she then became a little anxious when the visitors filed in after me. To give her some confidence, I held out my hand to take her paw and the sleepy babies yawned before cocking their heads with curiosity at the visitors.

Being on demand attention seekers, the kittens slowly came up to be cosseted and fawned over but Bonnie remained where she was. I then stepped back to give Marilyn a chance of getting to know Bonnie while Lucy and I concentrated on distracting the kittens.

Marilyn went over to Bonnie and held out her hand to her just as I had done. Without any hesitation Bonnie placed her paw in the waiting hand and their eyes locked. It was love at first sight.

Marilyn was really taken with her and said her large expressive eyes looked straight into her soul. Those expressive eyes that had touched me also touched Marilyn and I knew that if Marilyn decided to adopt Bonnie, she would be going to the best possible home she could have. It was only a matter of days before I had a call from Lucy that Marilyn wanted to adopt Bonnie.

The kittens were over 6 weeks old now and feeding on their own, so arrangements were made to have Bonnie vet worked before passing her on to Marilyn. I was ecstatic as well as saddened. I would really miss this little cat who had loved me heart and soul, but in rescue we have to remove ourselves from our own emotions and think about what is best for the cat. Having someone dote on her after she had been discarded was my reward for rescuing her. She would be going to a new life where she would be the centre of attention and the centre of Marilyn's world. How good was that.

Even so, a looming dread like a millstone hung around my neck. I would miss those hand to paw holds and those hugs. She was so special that I worried that losing her was going to create a large chasm in my heart that nothing else could fill. Or that's how it felt at the time. Through experience, I knew another cat would come along who would touch my heart, and with mother cats that happened rather often.

As it turned out, I didn't have long to wait or far to go to have my heart mended. Marilyn came to collect Bonnie, now named Molly, and took her home to start her new life.

Bonnie's kittens had started to take over the house causing all sorts of mischief so the kitten room was cleaned and sterilised after the previous kittens occupying the room were rehomed. They were also happy to include Matilda's baby in their games and a bond of friendship formed between them all.

Matilda joined the kittens in the larger kitten room and from observing some mothers in the past, it could have gone either way. She may have hissed and growled at the energetic interlopers, snapping and slapping them out of the way as they boldly bounded up to her. Instead, Matilda gathered the kittens into her care and mothered them as if they were her own. She loved it, relishing the role of caregiver, and now that she was in a healthy state, even allowing them to suckle from her. My love and admiration for her was growing and although she didn't show her gratitude in the way that Bonnie had, I knew she was finally feeling satisfied in her new role.

Matilda continued to care for the extra babies with her gentle demeanour. These confident kittens had drawn Matilda's baby into their circle, which made our task of bringing her out of her timid state so much easier. She was one of the gang and was gaining confidence alongside them. Soon it would be time for them all to have their vet work done and to advertise them. They were all quite photogenic

kittens with outgoing personalities so it wouldn't take long for them to find loving homes.

Having kittens around this age can be like having a house full of teenagers. Sometimes mother cats can get aggressive in their play and it is often a sign that they had done their natural duty and it was time for the babies to move on. With cats in the wild, an undesexed mother would leave to search for a mate and the cycle of breeding would begin again. She will often turn on the kittens to chase them away and make them fend for themselves.

Quite often when a mother with older babies is placed in a pen or carrier with her offspring for any length of time she will hiss and snarl at the babies. It happened regularly when we received a mother with kittens from the country who had spent some time travelling together to reach us. The mother, once released into a room, would hide away, with the confused babies not understanding why their lov-

ing mother had turned into a snarling, hissing stranger. It was mother nature working and sometimes they had to be separated from each other. In cases like this we would get the mother desexed as soon as possible and put her up for adoption. More often than not these young first-time mothers were still kittens themselves when they had the responsibilities of motherhood thrust upon them.

Matilda wasn't at all like this and cherished her time with these rowdy babies. Perhaps it was because of losing her own babies and the struggles she had to keep the remaining one and herself alive. She was always patient and gentle, and once again I was astounded that anyone could desert a cat with such a beautiful nature.

Like with many of the mother cats I rescued, food played an important part of rehabilitation and a starving cat never seemed to forget what starvation was like. Matilda was just grateful that someone was regularly feeding her and caring for her, so if that meant taking on extra kittens to look after,

so be it. Her needs and wants were simple and in return she was an easygoing cat. I would have to find a special home for her where she would never again be deserted or left hungry.

The kittens were ready to be vet worked and adopted, and as I had anticipated, it didn't take long for them to find loving homes. Matilda remained behind and the cloud of melancholy descended on her again. She still had her healthy appetite and appreciated the time I spent with her, gently patting her face and telling her what a wonderful mother she had been. She was so deserving of a loving home but being black and white in colour meant it would probably take longer to find that special home for her. Black and white cats were always a little harder to find homes for, as they didn't seem to be considered as pretty as other cats. With this in mind, we arranged a professional photographer to take her photo and bring out her best features. The photo did the trick and was also used in a calendar promoting pets. Someone had seen her photo with the description we gave and wanted to meet her.

As arranged a lovely lady came to view Matilda. She was kind, loved animals and Matilda seemed to take a shine to her. Her husband owned a horse racing stud and they wanted a cat for a companion as well as a mouser. Matilda, with her farming background, sounded like just what they were looking for, so with me feeling a mixture of sadness and gladness, Matilda went to her new home.

I always liked to know everything was going well in the new home so I would ring about a week later to make sure everything was alright and they were happy with the cat or kitten. With Matilda I need not have worried because she fitted straight in. The horse jockeys also had a soft spot for her and often went out of their way to give her a pat on their way to the track.

Over the years I had rehomed a few cats to horse trainers and people who owned horses, not only as mousers, but as loyal companions. It was born from centuries of cats guarding grain stores and keeping rat and mice numbers down. A perfect match.

When Lucy arrived again to help with the kittens, I was anxious to know how Molly was settling in with Marilyn.

My apprehension was relieved when Lucy informed me that Marilyn was besotted with Molly, and it seemed her affections were returned.

Once again, I posted an update on our Facebook page

to let everyone know that Bonnie was happily settled in her new home.

16 July 2015

We love happy endings. When Bonnie was found in a ditch beside a busy highway she had pretty much given up. She was very heavily pregnant, very hungry and had nowhere safe to go. The day she arrived with us she did nothing but shower us with love and affection, especially when food came regularly and in plentiful supply. She gave birth to her five babies who grew up in the foster home and delighted everyone with their kitten cuteness.

Bonnie herself went to an elderly lady who had spent most of her life looking after elderly relatives and once they passed on there wasn't much in her life to look forward to. Then Bonnie came into her life and this lady has dropped 10 years in age, is besotted with her companion and has a reason to get up every day. Bonnie never lets her owner out of her sight, always calling for her if she can't see her, and if she wants a pat she headbutts her leg. They sleep together, Bonnie has her head on the pillow next to her owner, and they share mealtimes…although Bonnie has hers in a dish on the floor. From where she came from to where she is now is a foster carer's dream and why we do what we do. It is the best feeling in the world seeing our guests transformed and established in their forever homes. Our mother cats deserve a home too.

When Marilyn had first come to visit Molly (then Bonnie), she knew straight away that she was going to be hers. To please the family, she went and visited other possible candidates for being her new companion, but her thoughts always returned to Molly. The first time the paw stretched out to touch her hand, the connection was made.

Molly went home with Marilyn and settled in as if she had always lived there. Marilyn had gone on a shopping spree buying her everything a cat could want, but of course Molly had decided that all she wanted was someone who loved her and fed her regularly. Her bedtime routine was to snuggle up with Marilyn on her bed, often curling up on her hip or spooning her if she turned over.

In the morning, at around 6.30 am, Molly would lightly kiss Marilyn on the eyelids while purring loudly. She would continue this until Marilyn acknowledged her and gave her a pat. This usually led to Marilyn rising and, of course, Molly would be fed.

After breakfast each morning, she patiently waits for Marilyn to clear up, then loves nothing better than to get comfortable on her lap and fall asleep.

If Marilyn is in another room out of sight, Molly would call out to her, anxious to know where she was. Marilyn would then reply, 'Here I am, Molly,' and Molly would happily join her in the room. They were never far from each other but just needed that little bit of reassurance that comes from close companionship.

When the travelling vet came to visit for Molly's regular check-up, he would gently remind Marilyn not to overfeed her or give her too many treats. She was growing rotund, with Molly always an eager recipient of the extras that Marilyn bestowed on her.

Molly has become so attached to Marilyn that she will

hide if anyone comes to visit. She is particularly afraid of men, which seems to suggest some man in her past may have done her harm or caused her to be abandoned.

When the visitors have gone, she will settle back with Marilyn, satisfied that her wonderful new life hasn't been disrupted.

As Marilyn states, there are so many wonderful things she could say about Molly, but she would then sound like one of those annoying mothers always bragging about their children.

Once she would have said, 'I live alone,' but now says, 'I live with Molly and we share our home together.'

Marilyn said that she had made a mistake in calling her Molly because her name really should be 'Princess'.

Who would have thought that the 'Guttersnipe' found in the ditch on a busy highway would have ended up being 'The Princess'. We wouldn't want it any other way.

Albie – the Store Cat

Our rescue was one of many that saved cats and kittens from country pounds, and as we specialised in mothers with babies and kittens, I was often tagged on a post for ones that may fit in with our rescue organisation.

Mostly we relied on a description and photo supplied by the staff at the pound and quite often their interpretation of a young kitten was exaggerated by several months.

One such kitten arrived, and when I checked his description it became obvious the 4-month-old kitten had doubled in size and age on the long journey to us. Along with other younger kittens came this black and white boy, about 8 months old, not quite adult in size, but definitely a teenager.

Space during kitten season was at a premium, with other foster carers fully occupied, so this big kitten had to stay with me, along with some smaller ones.

After the usual flea and worming treatments applied to all the new arrivals, they settled into the kitten room, which contained lots of toys, scratching posts and beds. All appeared to be well as they adjusted to their new temporary home.

At this stage Albie, as I named him, seemed to be like a big brother to the other kittens. It would be alright, I thought to myself as they all settled into the one bed, he will look after the little ones and make my life easier.

This happy thought was rudely interrupted by loud squealing emanating from the kitten room and on investigation of the source of the noise I discovered Albie holding down one of the kittens with one foot while batting away another at the same time. He was playing rough and kept tossing the younger playmates around as if he were bored with these wriggly toys.

My pleas to be nice to his younger playmates were completely ignored and it was clear this older teenager was going to cause a lot of trouble, especially for the younger kittens. He was a bully whose intention was to make life miserable for any kitten venturing anywhere near him, and for little kittens not long away from their mothers this was

not helping in their adjustment. He had to be removed from them but I had nowhere else available at short notice.

To ease the situation, I brought him out into the part of the house where my own resident cats belonged. At first, he enjoyed his freedom outside the kitten room, but being a totally self-obsessed, in-your-face, attention seeking cat, it didn't take long for him to annoy our cats.

We had three cats, two who were quite elderly and just wanted a quiet life. They showed utter disdain for any fosters who happened to cross their paths.

To Albie, this was a challenge, with him using standover tactics to make them uncomfortable. Being hissed at was like pressing a button in his brain and all he wanted was for them to run so he could chase them. He was having so much fun and no amount of scolding by me was going to deter him.

As we had a large garden, we had a cat flap so our cats could escape from the antics of the kittens who always seemed to think that a cat bed was an offer to feel at home.

It took Albie all of 20 seconds to work out that the cat flap meant freedom and our escaping resident cats were horrified when he came charging out of the flap to join them. On giving chase it didn't take long for one to scramble up a high tree with Albie hanging on a branch underneath wondering whether to continue up or look for easier prey.

He had such a smug look of determination as if to say, 'See, I can get rid of them for you. Now you will just have me!'

Albie wasn't a bad cat; in fact, he was utterly adorable and would curl around your legs as if you were the most important person in his life. It's just that he was selfish and didn't want to share you with anyone else.

Even our poor dog was victim to his plotting to rid the house of any pet except himself. He would hang on to her tail as if it were a merry-go-round, letting go once she whipped around to give him a good nip, then jump up on the kitchen bench out of dog reach. You could almost see the edges of his lips curled up with glee as the frustrated dog would bark her annoyance.

Quite often on the weekends we would laze around in the morning reading the newspaper and this was a time we often bonded with the foster kittens. For Albie it seemed like a good time to join in, except the newspaper held up to read would be used to make an entrance close to your face. He couldn't understand why a flimsy piece of paper would be between him and the person he wanted attention from so he would pounce into it in an effort to break the barrier. Quite often he would achieve his target with the newspaper

being split as if it had been struck by lightning. He would then place two front legs on your chest and stare into your face until you scratched his ears and gave in to his attention seeking ways. It was hard to be annoyed with him because he was so funny, but at the same time he needed some discipline.

The first thing to do was book Albie in for his vet work, and being around 8 months old he would be developing sex hormones which possibly contributed to his domineering ways.

He was the perfect patient at the vet's with the staff all saying how well behaved and friendly he was. My guess was that he came from a farm or rural area with space and that his overbearing selfishness was born from competition with other farm pets and animals. He was fearless and seemed to cope with anything, except being loaded into a carrier and taken away.

His recovery at home was quick and he was soon back to his usual self, especially when it came to seeking attention. I really needed to find him a home but with an older black and white kitten who would need to be the only cat, this was probably going to take some time.

We had an arrangement with the local PETstock store in Somerville on the Mornington Peninsula where we took some of our kittens available for adoption and placed them into a cat enclosure in the store. The enclosure was spacious with netting on all sides and room for a large cat scratching tree, along with other toys and litter trays. People wanting to adopt a kitten could come and view them, then talk to the foster carer or staff about adoption. We always advertised when they would be at the store on our Facebook page and usually had a good response from the public.

The staff were really wonderful and knew how much the foster carers worried about whether their kittens would be going to a good home, so always took a lot of care with them when they came into the store. I wondered if the cat enclosure would be a good place to put Albie during the day, so he could get all the attention he wanted without causing stress on my pets and the other foster kittens.

A phone call with Lauren, the store manager, eased my concerns when she said they would be delighted to have Albie in the store. My cats and dog would also be delighted. We decided to trial it to see how he went and I would bring him home at night then take him back the next day.

My initial concerns were eased considerably on learning that Albie was on a cat harness and being led around the

store by one of the staff members. He was not so keen on sitting on his own in the cat enclosure when there were so many people around the store who could give him attention, so he worked his magic on the staff.

By placing him in the harness on a long lead, he had a bit of freedom but could be controlled if necessary. This

seemed to suit Albie, and being the smart cat he is, he saw the situation as being an opportunity for getting the attention he craved. A captive audience was waiting patiently to be served.

Placing himself on the countertop, he then sauntered over to where the front customer was and sat there waiting to be patted. Whether the customer liked cats or not made no difference to Albie; in fact, he would stare at them directly in the face as if to ask, 'What's wrong with you and what is your problem with cats.' Inevitably he would win the day, with most people obliging by giving his ears a scratch or his head a pat. He didn't mind which, so long as he got his way.

The only place at home I could put Albie at night was in a small bathroom with a dodgy latch where he could be kept away from our cats and the foster kittens. Quite often he would scratch away at the door latch until it gave way, giving him access to the master bedroom and the bed. There he would place himself, comfortably ensconced between the pillows as if it were his natural domain. When I sternly asked him what he was doing, he would lift his head as if to say, 'Are you stupid? I'm waiting for you.'

He was not at all pleased when shown his bed in the bathroom, but his activities during the day must have exhausted him as he soon settled down for the night.

Albie was quite happy to be taken to the pet store again, and after regaling them with the stories of his attempts to sleep in our room, the staff offered to keep him at the store overnight. After all, he would have free rein on the lead for most of the day and the cat enclosure would be safe for him overnight. This arrangement seemed to be the best for the moment until he found his new forever home.

To help us find that perfect home I started to advertise on our Facebook page that Albie would be in residence at the pet store for anyone wishing to meet him with the prospect of giving him a home.

February 2018

Albie will be at PETstock Somerville on Wednesday 21 Feb and will probably be lazing on the counter checking out the customers or on the harness taking a staff member for a walk. Come along and meet this lovable boy and if you own a farm or a lot of land for him to run around in, you might be the right person to adopt him. He will be lazing around from 9.00 am until 4.00 pm.

This first post received a lukewarm response but I was sure we would find the right home if I kept advertising him.

Mr Personality is charming all the staff and customers at PETstock in Somerville. Come along and meet Albie and help the staff have a break from all his attention seeking.

This post received more attention with people commenting that they had seen Albie in the store and it was true, he sits on the counter seeking pats and head scratches.

Albie was not one for being held for long so cuddles were out of the question. He would stretch his body stiffly and hold his head away with a message that was loud and clear that cuddling was to be on his terms.

The next day I again posted another account of Albie at the store.

Mr Character Albie will be gracing the counter and expecting lots of pats at PETstock in Somerville today from 10.30 am until 4.00 pm. Come along and say hello to Albie and if you would like an in-your-face, not to be ignored cat who needs lots of room to run around and who thinks he is a dog, then please consider giving him a home. He is overconfident in many respects so would be best as the only cat but loves human company.

By now Albie was starting to attract attention, with people coming from all over the shire to visit the cat at the store. Children would drag their parents along saying, 'We want to meet Albie,' and then line up to give him a pat. Albie loved all this attention but there now were limits to his availability. When there was a lull in customers he would climb up to the top shelf where the comfy dog beds were and have a sleep. After all, even showmen need to sleep.

After bringing him home from time to time after his showtime at the store, it was decided that he would stay permanently overnight in the cat enclosure. He would mostly sleep after his exhausting day and at night would be visited by the resident store cat who was kept as a mouser. They would touch noses, but if given the chance, Albie would push the mouser out the door and take her place. He wasn't one for sharing the limelight even if it meant chasing mice at night.

My next post on the now well-known 'Albie the Store Cat' drew lots of comments especially from children coming to see him.

Albie will be at the counter at PETstock Somerville today and all this week interviewing anyone who meets his criteria of being a prospective new owner. He will be taking pats and compliments from 10.00 am until closing time but needs to take naps occasionally in that time. (Cats need their beauty sleep too.) If you have a farm or room for him to run around, then do pop down to the store and make an appointment to be interviewed by him.

The next time I went to the store to check on Albie I was greeted at the door by one of the staff members who announced that they had a permanent home for Albie. With great excitement I exclaimed what wonderful news that was and what were the new owners like?

She sheepishly looked at me and said, 'We are going to adopt him,' meaning the store. He was going to be their store cat, but the owner would be the store manager Lauren. He would remain at the store for much of the time but would be going home with Lauren who had a small farm with lots of animals and horses. They owned dogs but no cat so Albie would virtually be another dog. He would love that.

I was absolutely thrilled to hear of this arrangement and suggested the local newspaper do an article about him. After all, he was a very special cat, one of a kind really.

My next post on our Facebook page was to break the news that Albie had a home.

28 February 2018

It had to happen...the PETstock Somerville staff have fallen in love with Albie so he is staying. This funny, quite extraordinary one-of-a-kind cat will now grace the counter waiting to be patted and told what a gorgeous boy he is.

So come on down and say hello to Albie, but he has chosen his family and they all adore him.

The local *Leader* newspaper ran a story about Albie, saying that: 'Albie's got purrrsonality. And it's earned him a new home and a full-time job. The eight-month-old moggy was recently taken to PETstock Somerville as part of a cat adoption program. But staff fell in love with the outgoing feline.' (9 March 2018, 'Staff at Sommerville store running cat adoption program feline the love for outgoing moggy.')

As a result of the newspaper article Albie became a star, with people coming from all over to visit the store and meet him.

Lauren, the store manager, was never one of those children growing up who would hound her parents for a cat. She loved cats but was more of a 'dog person'. When the opportunity came to partner with our rescue organisation, she was very enthusiastic, ensuring the kittens and cats would have the best of care while at the store. This arrangement worked very well with our rescue because many of our foster carers were single women or had children and I was never very comfortable with people coming to their homes to view the foster cats or kittens. They were raised in a loving environment with all the distractions that a busy household would give them and people loved adopting them because they would adjust so well in their new homes.

Having the store where viewing could take place, the kittens would get used to people visiting, as well as dogs and the usual noise of store activities. There were plenty of cocoon beds if a shy kitten wanted to hide away but any moment the staff had free was spent cuddling and petting. The staff were just an added extension to our foster carers and they always loved having the little guests in the store, always keeping us up to date with any interest shown.

Albie going into the store was not so he could build up his confidence but to give my animals a break and me a chance to get on with some other work.

When Lauren first met Albie she knew he would be trouble – but in a good way.

Albie had no intention of spending his time sitting about in the cat enclosure and lured the staff into bringing him out into the store with them. They decided to place him on a harness with a long lead to see how it went. Albie took all of two seconds to think he owned the store, taking charge at the counter where he was assured of getting attention.

Our Facebook posts had drawn attention to Albie and one day a lovely lady with young children came in with the view of adopting him. She thought he would be the perfect fit for her family and after asking lots of questions of Lauren, the lady said she needed to talk to her husband first about adopting him.

On hearing this news, Lauren's usually happy face suddenly changed when it dawned on her that they would be losing Albie. The home sounded perfect for him but this dog lover's heart was breaking. She couldn't bear to part with him, and it seemed none of the staff wanted him to go either. When the lady was leaving the store, Lauren said to her that there would be no guarantees that Albie would still be available when she came back. She would have to take that risk.

When I came to check on Albie and Lauren advised that he was staying with her, I realised I couldn't think of a better home for this extraordinary cat. Lauren had a property with lots of animals, horses, dogs and now she was becoming a cat owner, with one who thought he was better than a dog!

Lauren's oldest daughter had always pestered her for a cat and until now Lauren had always resisted. The store had plenty of felines for them to cuddle so there was no need for them to own one.

There was great excitement when Albie came home with Lauren. At last the children would have a cat to add to the other pets they had. Albie would sleep on her oldest daughter's bed, and she would help to feed him and look after him.

Albie viewed this situation as not up to his expectations. There was another, younger, child who seemed to be missing out and in typical cat form, Albie decided that his sleeping partner would be the youngest in the family. It didn't matter how many times he was taken off the bed and placed with the older daughter, he would always return to the other bed. A week later the youngest daughter would be calling Albie to bed and they would curl up together. Every morning she would come out of her room saying, 'Mum, Albie snores so loud. How do you make him stop?'

When Lauren was dressed for work, Albie would see the uniform and decide whether he wanted to go to work for the day or stay at home. Some days he would hide away, which meant he didn't want to go, and other days he would be at the front door waiting to go. He had his little car seat attachment and would sit on the back seat ready for his day at work.

When Albie arrived with Lauren, he would go out the back of the store where interesting things were happening. When the bales of hay were being unloaded, Albie would go up high on a ledge, then hop on top of the bales to check them out. The truck drivers would always ask where the quality control officer was.

As the store cat, Albie's main plan for the day was to meet and greet customers, but sometimes his plans were altered by dogs who thought cats were inferior beings that needed to be chased. One day a young Husky dog came into the store with its owner who said the dog had never seen a cat before and she wasn't sure how he would react.

It was as if Albie had been listening to the conversation, and he sauntered towards the dog, then lay down on the floor just out of reach. The Husky tried desperately to get near him, but Albie rolled around the floor showing off as he knew the dog couldn't reach him. He then jumped up on the counter with a self-satisfied smug look as if to say, 'Dog done and dusted!'

Another part of Albie's day was to attend puppy school, and being superior to playful puppies was something he relished. There was also a class for adult dogs so Albie wisely kept at leash length during these sessions. He would sit down out of reach and tease them, daring them to come any closer. One day a Greyhound decided that a cat was for chasing but Albie stood his ground and stared him out, resulting in the Greyhound backing down. Albie never took his eyes from him but settled out of reach just in case he needed to escape. He loved to get a reaction out of dogs…and people.

Albie fitted in well with the farm animals and on his days off with Lauren would accompany her to feed the horses. He even sat on the horse's rump as she walked it around the paddock. There he was king of his paradise.

Although he was a cat, Albie thought he was a dog and loved to show his superiority with the resident Border Collie. She was happy for him to be around but had no interest in playing with him. He would hide behind the wall and jump out at her, then hang on to her back legs while she tried to walk past.

If she was sleeping on her bed, he would come and try to get in with her, knowing full well it would make her leave the bed. Then he would sit there with a smug look on his face.

Albie loved to be involved in whatever was happening, whether it was housework or emptying the dishwasher. He would climb in behind the trays and tap the spinning arm as if trying to work out the mechanics.

If anyone was cooking, he would be there to supervise.

He always loved the element of surprise and would jump out at anyone going past the microwave. You could almost see his lips curl up as the victim squealed with shock.

After a hard day at work meeting and greeting people and dogs, Albie loves nothing better than going home with Lauren. At first he wasn't much of a lap cat and wanted to be involved in whatever was going on, but with time he has turned into a cuddly lap cat. If Lauren was working he would push the laptop off her lap so he could curl up and have a sleep. When it was time for bed, Albie would be waiting there, ready to snuggle.

Lauren wasn't really a 'cat person' and only had dogs before, but Albie has turned the tables on her and her family.

As she says, 'Albie is one of a kind and we couldn't imagine life without him.'

He is quite an extraordinary cat.

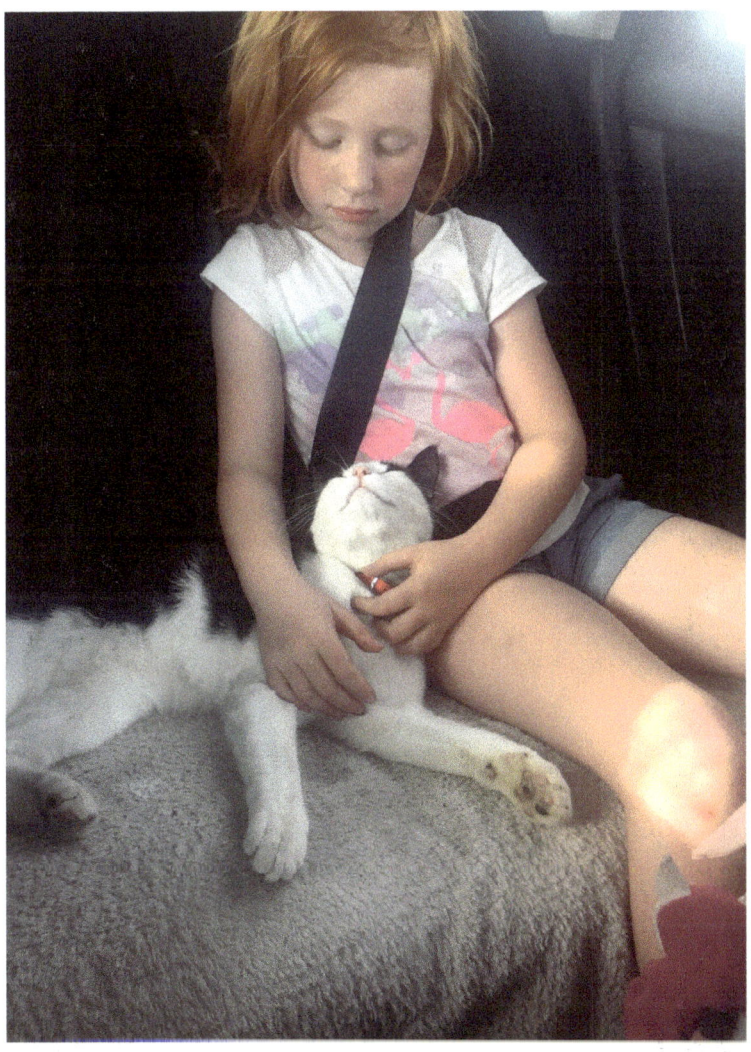

Letters from a Little Black Cat

One of the most difficult things we have to cope with when we rescue cats is having to deal with the problems caused by animal hoarders. Cat hoarders are possibly some of the worst. It is probably where the term 'crazy cat lady' stems from, and it doesn't always come to anyone's attention until someone enters a home or dwelling to see what is actually going on.

Hoarders are sometimes diagnosed with mental health issues. The problem with animal hoarders is they want to continue to rescue more and more. They believe they are the only ones who can save the world. Quite often the animals end up in a worse situation than they were in before, so disease and behavioural issues are prevalent.

Cat hoarders can vary in severity but the outcome for the cats can be the same. They place the cats in a situation where they have to fight for food, the litter trays are sparse and overflowing with faeces and the stench is unbearable. Cats, being extremely clean animals, suffer particularly because they are confined to one area or room, with no fresh air or sunshine. Quite often they are kept in darkened rooms with curtains and blinds drawn to keep prying eyes away from the hoard. It is pure hell for cats and in particular for those who are trying to raise babies.

It was from one such place in the country that we rescued multiple nursing cats and kittens. We tried to get out as many as we could possibly manage. However, it can be a fraught time especially for the hoarder and coaxing them to give up the animals takes a lot of patience and urging. In the pounds and shelters we worked with, we came across many hoarding situations, and bringing the animals around to trust and making them better takes a lot of time and resources. Sometimes they are too disease-ridden, inbred or damaged, and euthanasia is the only option to stop further suffering. It is so very sad.

After rescuing these mothers and kittens, we distributed them around to our team of foster carers.

I took two very young mother cats, one with four kittens and another with just one kitten. She had given birth to three but two had died with just one kitten surviving.

We placed the first mother in the bathroom with her four babies and the other in another room away from them. The nursing mother had settled in well but the other mother and her single baby were struggling and were both in a state of distress.

As an experienced foster carer, I soon worked out that the young mother with one kitten had no milk and her little one was starving. Quickly I took the hungry baby to the other mother cat and placed it to the back of her suckling kittens so she wouldn't notice.

This mother cat did notice but straightaway she licked the baby and encouraged it to feed from her. It was obvious the mother knew this baby either from the hoarding situation or she was already accustomed to simply feeding any baby that needed her milk. She was quite a skinny little cat with Abyssinian markings but she had the most gentle, nurturing nature. These hungry babies were being attended to so I knew I had to make sure the mother had plenty of good food to generate the milk she needed.

The other mother cat, tabby and white, and barely a kitten herself, was very friendly. As she had no milk, I felt the best thing for her was to have her desexed and placed into our adoption program as quickly as possible.

Having kept her separated from the new feeding arrangements overnight, it became apparent next morning that the little tabby and white cat was stressing and missing her baby. I opened the door to her room and then the door to the room where the other mother and her baby were being kept. I waited to see what would happen. I was unsure of what the reaction would be from the nursing mother as I watched with apprehension, ready to act if needed. It could have easily gone all pear-shaped with snarling and hissing, but instead there was an enthusiastic, happy greeting. The two cats smothered each other with lashings of licks and nudges, followed by a thorough cleaning session of all the kittens. It was obvious these two mother cats shared a bond with their babies and they delighted in helping each other.

One mother cat fed while the other cleaned, top, bottom and in between. They then groomed each other with love and satisfaction in their eyes.

All seemed to go well so I decided that separating these two mothers that shared their mothering duties might not be in their best interests, so the little tabby and white mum stayed.

As happens so often when we take on new mums and kittens, we never know the full picture of what we are dealing with. Unfortunately, they succumbed to the dreaded cat flu, something we often had to contend with. It was probably carried with them from the hoarding home and then the stress of their poor condition and being transported down to us would have brought it on.

They became very sick and required medication and

around the clock watching. The mother cats slowly came through it and one by one we nursed the babies carefully through their illness. Cat flu has different effects and a lot depends on the health of the cat or kittens and whether their immune system can fight it. There are also different strains of cat flu but the treatment is mostly the same. It was a worrying time watching such young kittens with distressed snuffles and watery, encrusted eyes. I had seen so many kittens not survive and I unfortunately have many little mounds of earth in my garden to show how final it can be.

It took several weeks of nurturing and medication for the kittens to regain their strength. Having two mothers doting on them would no doubt have expedited their recovery. It was the right decision to keep them all together.

We noticed that two of the kittens, Ramona and Maya, were not gaining weight and were still suffering from the after-effects of cat flu. The two mothers had their appetites back and although they were still sneezing, the milk was flowing freely. The other three kittens seemed to be gaining in strength but still needed to have their eyes wiped and were still snuffling. Along with medication we also used a vaporiser with steam to help with breathing. Everything was being done to get this little family better.

Ramona and Maya were still not growing and I began to be concerned about their development. After another visit to the vet for more medication and vitamin gels to stimulate their appetite, I decided to separate them from the others so they could receive more attention and changed their diet to meat I had cooked for them. The warm roast meat chopped up did stimulate their appetites which is what I was hoping for. All good signs.

Finally, after weeks of medication and care, the two little mother cats who had raised their babies together were going to be rehomed together. Their struggles to survive in the hoarding house, their illness and caring for their kittens would all be forgotten. For a rescuer, that is the best reward for all our hard work and efforts, and the photos I later received from their new owners, of the cats happily stretched out together on a bed, was truly gratifying. I was so chuffed and proud at the same time. The other kittens recovered and found homes easily after their vet work, but I still had Ramona and Maya to care for.

On the new diet, Ramona had developed quite an appetite and made up for lost time in great growth spurts, but poor little Maya lagged behind in spite of her efforts to eat all her food. She was still tiny but had an extended belly which was very concerning.

Using a large syringe, the vet would draw out about a quarter cup full of fluid from her and once again we would put her on antibiotics to see if her little body could beat whatever was causing this.

Ramona was constantly tugging at her ear and after ascertaining it wasn't due to fleas or mites, I began to worry about what might be afflicting her. She didn't have the lack of energy that Maya had; in fact, it was quite the opposite and in the room I had placed them, Ramona was being a naughty kitten. She would climb up the curtains, sitting on the top rail as if to defiantly dare me to catch her. Although she was very affectionate to Maya, she also tried to play with her and became very frustrated when Maya cried out in surrender in a game of tussle. Ramona was bored and needed more stimulation than her lethargic sister to play with, but I wasn't prepared to let her play with my cats or any other kittens. Just in case.

Maya's belly was extending again and she wasn't growing or gaining weight. I duly took her back to the vet's to have her belly syringed again. After weighing Maya and discovering she was losing weight and not gaining it, a decision had to be made. Maya was not going to get better and she was going to die, fairly soon from all indications. She had all the symptoms of FIP, a fatal disease for most kittens. I had to give the vet the go ahead to end her life and the decision was killing me. I knew he was right, all the indications were there for me to see, but I was struggling to give him the go ahead. Death is so final and I had seen so much death that I wanted Maya to survive, to beat this, to live.

After wrapping Maya's body up to bury in my garden, I hurried out of the vet's before succumbing to waves of sobbing. I cried and cried for that darling little girl who had tried so hard. I cried for all the others I couldn't save as well and my shoulders shook with the release of tears. It is something we who rescue sometimes do because we are so passionate about what we do. One little soul amongst the many who are killed in pounds and shelters across the country doesn't seem fair but we can only block out so many deaths. They do catch up with you and one stands out to attack your stored up tears. Maya did that to me, along with a few others over the years.

Maya was buried along with all the other little babies that didn't make it and I made a point to plant some pretty flowers on that spot.

Ramona was alone in the room now and seemed to sense my great sorrow at losing Maya. She had a way of knowing the intense sadness I was suffering and would bury herself into my lap while gazing lovingly into my eyes. She was such a special little kitten and I adored her.

The vet thought it wise that I brought Ramona into the clinic for a thorough check-up. Ramona was rapidly gaining weight, her sneezing had stopped and she had a glossy coat and shiny eyes. I was certain all would be fine but mentioned to the vet her tugging at her ear.

On examination of the ear, the vet discovered a large polyp was growing inside, probably as a result of the cat flu. He would need to operate on it by opening up her ear, and depending on whether it was growing down or up, cut it out. The whole left side of her ear would need to be half cut away to give access. A difficult and tricky operation. If the growth was coming up the ear, it could be removed. If it was growing down and attaching to her brain, she would have to be euthanised.

Looking at the vet in sheer horror at the possibility of losing this little girl as well, I asked if there were other options. There weren't any and we had to take this direction to discover if she lived or died. I felt sick, overwhelmed with emotions that I was struggling to contain.

A date was set, with this major operation imprinted in my head as well as in my diary.

The day arrived and after prepping her for her operation I gave her one last cuddle before handing her over to the vet nurses.

The hours ticked by, made slower by my constant clock watching. Would I be picking Ramona up in a carrier or a body bag?

After several hours, the call came, with my vet telling me it had all gone well and that Ramona was in recovery. I could scarcely hear what he was saying because my pounding heart was beating so loudly and my brain wasn't computing the intricacies of the operation. All I knew was that she had made it and was going to be alright. My clever, beautiful little Ramona was coming home.

After listening to the instructions from the vet on how to care for Ramona, I brought her home and carefully laid her in her bed in her room. Her head was heavily bandaged with just the eyes, nose and mouth appearing beneath the shroud of white. She would also need to have the Elizabethan collar on to stop her pawing at the bandages and undoing the stitches around her ear. She really did look a sorry sight but stitches would heal, bandages and collar would be removed and fur would grow back. She was going to be alright, of that I was certain. She was such a good patient, and after months of cat flu treatment, pill taking and medicine, she seemed to take it as normal that I would be opening her mouth to push something in for her to swallow. It was as if she understood I was trying to make her better and the cuddles she was dispensing to me seemed to confirm that.

After a few weeks it was time to take the bandage off to see how the ear was healing. My vet had done such an excellent job and he was as pleased as I was to see it was mending. She would look a bit strange for a while as there was a large scar where the ear had been cut and drawn down, but before we knew it her fur started to grow back and she would be back to her pretty old self.

The final vet check confirmed the polyp had gone and there was no further regrowth. She was now desexed and ready to go to her own forever home.

Many foster carers find rehoming their kittens the hardest part of fostering and I would agree with that. We pour our heart and soul into turning them around, to make them trusting, affectionate, loving, and then handing them over to someone else to love is hard. We always worry that they will feel safe, that they will be cared for properly, that the new owner will love them as much as we love them. There is always the dread that all our hard work will be in vain and the numbers of cats surrendered and abandoned suggests it happens quite a lot.

I had to find the best home for Ramona, even if it took a while. She was quite happy with us and would remain until I was certain she would go to a good home. Plus, there was always the worry that if she wasn't properly cared for, her illness might return, a possibility I didn't want to encounter.

After taking lots of photos of Ramona in different poses I found one which I thought captured her sweet nature and wrote a caption which I thought might attract the right new owner.

Ramona was oblivious to all of this and continued to snuggle in my arms, purring as if I was the most important

thing in her life. Now I was going to betray that trust by giving her to someone else.

With no calls forthcoming to adopt her I was beginning to think Ramona was going to stay with us, and the longer she stayed, the harder it would be to let her go. People may have been put off because she was black, stemming back to a silly superstition about black cats. That she had been sick and needed a polyp removed might have also been a factor, or that she was now nearly 5 months old and not the cute little kitten that people desire. With patience I was sure the right person would come along.

A call did come. Someone was after a black cat and didn't mind that she wasn't a small kitten; in fact, they preferred her a bit older. They also didn't mind that she had had a major ear operation and that she had also been very sick as a young kitten. She was better now as far as we could tell and the vet was quite happy for her to go to her new home. I was getting very excited that this might be the right home for Ramona, but at the same time I felt an overwhelming dread. I would miss her terribly.

Jane made the long journey down to meet Ramona and said it was for her parents who lived on a farm. They had 10 acres where they kept horses, had a dog and wanted a black cat. They previously had a black cat but it had died a few years ago and they felt they wanted another – and they particularly wanted a black cat. Ramona seemed just what they were hoping for. Talking to Jane was almost like talking to an old friend and we clicked straight away. I felt very comfortable with what she was saying about her family but I wanted to be sure and talk to them separately.

Michael phoned me and I interrogated him on what he would be offering Ramona in her new home. She was very dear to me and had been through so much, and I wanted him to be sure that Ramona was the right kitten for them. She would mostly be an inside cat although she would have access to outside and she would have her own bed in their bedroom at night. Michael assured me that she would want for nothing and that they loved cats, particularly his wife Jan.

That was all I could hope for so arrangements were made for Jane to come down again to collect Ramona and take her to her new home.

It was lovely meeting Jane again and my instincts told me Ramona was going to a wonderful new life. Even so, I wanted to be sure everything was going well and asked Jane to promise to let me know if there were any problems. Ramona had been through so much and I was concerned that any stress in a new environment would be detrimental to her adjusting.

Michael was as good as his word and I received a very welcome email from him telling me that Ramona was settling in well.

1/5/2014

Dear Joy,

Thanks a million for Ramona who is settling in remarkably quickly. She and Stella the whippet kelpie cross have been kissing each other although somewhat tentatively. Mona has managed to find every cobweb in the house – good job it is just me, Jan and Jane to see the place needs dusting. Will report again in a few days.

Warmest thanks,

Michael A.

7/5/2014

Dear Michael,

As you have had Ramona for nearly a week now I'm just checking that you are happy with everything and that she has settled into her new home.

Before I send in the change of ownership form, do you want to change her name as that is what will be recorded on the microchip?

Thank you again for giving Ramona a home and I look forward to your return reply.

Kind regards

Joy

Peninsula Cat Rescue Inc.

LETTERS FROM A LITTLE BLACK CAT

8/5/2014

Dear Joy,

Thanks for your email; you beat me to it. We seem to have fallen into the habit of calling her Monny. She is fully settled in, eating voraciously and fully comfortable with everything. She now wears a shiny blue collar with a bell and she loves it. She seems to prefer women and is totally addicted to Jan, spending as much time as she can cuddling and being cuddled by her and a little more diffident with me. She has been outside investigating and is fascinated with all the birds around. She makes her own way back in but responds when called. She is absolutely perfect and I see no prospect at all of Jan and Jane parting with her, let alone me. She is very like our second last cat Lettie who died a couple of years ago at 16 and a half so we hope she will have as long and happy a life with us. We would be obliged if you could attend to the change of ownership for us. I will get Jane to send a photo.

With warmest thanks,

Michael A.

Dear Joy,

This is me at Ashgrove.

Love Monny (Ramona)

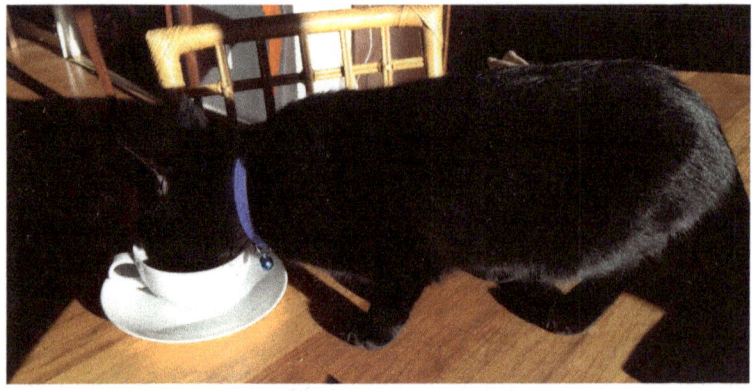

I know I shouldn't do this but it was only Michael's cup.

Love Monny

I like my tea weak and black.

I was ecstatic that things were going well at Ashgrove farm for Ramona and maybe in my enthusiasm I let my usual decorum down with a rather silly, flippant reply. I'm not quite sure why I did it but talking to Michael on the phone and reading about the cobwebs in his first email, I sensed he had a sense of humour. I pressed the send button with a great deal of apprehension.

8/5/2014

Dear Miss Ramona or Monny, as you are now affectionately called.

Where are your manners Miss 'I can get away with it cause I'm cute'?

Did you not learn anything in your foster home?

You grew up there with your brothers and sisters so there is no excuse for jumping on tables and helping yourself to a cup of tea!!

You did not come from a bad home where you were neglected, starved and unloved! No…you had your foster family cooing over you and had the best of everything. Well, you did have to share with all the other waifs but that is no excuse for thinking you are human, now you have a home of your own.

Please show more gratitude to your new owners by not helping yourself to their food and drinks, and no more jumping on tables in case things are more interesting from up there.

Your loving ex foster mum. XXX

p.s. …You do look very sweet with your new collar. X

A return email arrived and my great state of apprehension dissipated with the reply.

9/5/2014

Dear ex Mum,

I didn't know that that man was writing to you and getting Jane to photograph me in compromising posture. I am devastated that you might doubt my manners – if Michael leaves his cup on the table to go and feed horses – things I am yet to see, what do you expect – after all, Jane encouraged me.

Now let me tell you about this lunatic place:

Did Jane tell you she doesn't live here all the time but only visits every two or three days? Did she tell you that Jan and Michael are really old and only watch ABC or SBS?

I think you know that the dog is black like me – I think we will get on but for the moment I maintain nun-like reserve.

What is this about ping pong balls – they rush about the polished floor and are so difficult to catch; but I am quick enough to catch them.

There is a thing called outside which is very strange. There is green stuff that is sort of wet and squidgy that has all sorts of little live things in it, I think they call it grass. There are also lots of birds who come really close but I don't think I will try to tackle the big white ones with funny yellow stand up hair and very nasty looking noses. Silly Michael takes them a cup of black stuff and puts it in a sort of contraption on which they stand – could they be eating it? OMG!

Thank you for sending the feeding regime because if you hadn't I would probably be eating horse feed – all I hear is 'I will feed the horses.' Can you imagine?

Despite all this I am very happy and think that I might be able to get this place to order.

Wish me luck,

Your loving foster daughter,

Monny

LETTERS FROM A LITTLE BLACK CAT

13/5/2014

Dearest Monny,

If you learnt anything in the foster home it was good table manners. So I was a bit disappointed to hear that you had let our good reputation down by taking the first opportunity to jump on tables and drink weak black tea left lying around. Taking advantage of your new owners in the first week is not how we brought you up!!

I also hope that when you are skittling ping pong balls along the wooden floors you would be good enough to use your tail as a duster as you go and be a bit useful. After all you need to earn your keep and not just selfishly lie about expecting to be fed on call or when you raise your meow!!

Also, make sure you eat up all your food, especially cooked chicken drumsticks which I know is your favourite (no bones) and lay off eating too many dry biscuits. They are bad for your figure and you don't know where they've been or what is in them.

If you want to clean your teeth, then raw chicken necks or wings are best, we don't want bad breath and dirty teeth when snuggling up to Jan, Jane and Michael.

When drinking your lactose free milk please do not make slurping noises and especially don't drop any on the floor for someone to slip on.

Remember that your mother was probably an Abyssinian with royal blood, neglected to start with but honoured for her beauty and charms in her new home. As for your father, he was probably a dark horse who charmed the ladies then left them with wild abandon. We won't mention him again!!

Always show your appreciation by purring loudly and gaze adoringly at your new family, just like you did with us.

Don't show favouritism towards the female humans as the male also deserves your attention and love. Especially Michael who will teach you about being wise in the outdoors while he feeds the horses. And please do be careful around horses...they are much bigger than you and if one steps on you, or God forbid kicks you, it will hurt. You have had enough stitches and bandages for one lifetime so I'm sure you don't want any more.

Also be careful of birds...especially big birds. Remember how you used to watch the Kookaburras and Myna birds in your foster home from a safe distance behind a window. You would be wise to do the same in your new home as one peck from them might send you off to the vet's for more bandages and stitches.

If Michael, Jan and Jane are watching TV, you could join in by showing them how clever you are at sports, especially downhill skiing. In fact, it was quite remiss of the Olympic selectors not to pick you as you were quite the champion and very entertaining trying to run down and catch the skiers. Tell them you are also partial to a bit of tennis watching but can't quite fathom where the ball has gone. You always run around behind the TV but it doesn't seem to be there. Very strange that.

Darling girl, your foster family misses you but your foster buddies don't. They are jealous that you have a family who cares about you and you don't have to share, except with a dog but she doesn't count.

So please, no more bad manners and look after your new family.

Love from your ex foster mum. xx

13/5/2014

Darling ex Mum

I was thinking of you on Mother's Day, I hope you had a happy day. I have been at Ashgrove now for nearly two weeks and love it, especially Jan who is just so warm to cuddle with and she makes me purr a lot. Did you know that I have the poshest litter tray with its own little door that flaps up when I enter – it is soooo private when I have to go which is very nice indeed. Michael and Jane were shocked at your suggestion that I use my tail for dusting. Jane says it is far too beautiful for that. I don't need to earn my keep because you know that Jane is in the entertaining industry so all I have to do is entertain; and you know how good I am at that. My favourite sleeping place is on the piano stool which has an antique camel's cushion which is just so comfy and I can imagine I am an Arabic princess riding a camel which is very exciting – perhaps my Abyssinian blood lines coming through? The food here is very good and Jane has just brought me some more lactose free milk which I have always loved as you well know. There haven't been any drumsticks yet but Michael has promised me some soon – yum yum yum.

Although it is very nice here, I haven't forgotten your kind and loving care.

Much love,

Monny (short for Ramona)

17/5/2014

Dearest Monny,

How sweet it was of you to think of me on Mother's Day. As you know, one of the greatest pleasures I have is to see a mother cat and her babies go from being hungry, neglected and unwanted into glossy, happy, healthy families in the foster home. We adore every one of you and love to see the babies transform into loving little cats with their individual personalities.

Your own mother was a pleasure to have and she never failed to show us her gratitude and love. After attending to you and your siblings, she always adored having her ears and chin gently scratched and being told how beautiful she was. I think you take after her in that regard.

You and your siblings were very special in that you had two mums to look after you and the newspapers even wrote a piece about you (although they were not totally accurate but we won't let the truth get in the way of a good story).

I'm so glad that you love snuggling up with Jan and purring. I bet you tell her how special she is with that adoring look you give.

It sounds as though you are being spoilt with your own private litter tray and having a special antique seat to sleep on.

Just remember that although you enjoy entertaining everyone, it might be best not to sing any opera while near the piano or snore while on the seat. Jane may not think that sort of entertaining is worth promoting or sharing with anyone else.

I am very pleased to hear you are making yourself at home and feeling relaxed. Some of your foster mates have also been adopted and we all hope they are as happy as you.

I've added a photo of your mother with her babies just to show Jan, Michael and Jane just how beautiful your mum was and how she doted on you all. I think you have inherited her gentle eyes if not the colour of her coat.

Stay happy, sweetheart, and enjoy your new home and owners.

From your loving ex foster mum. xx

1/6/2014

Dearest Aunty Joy,

Michael says that the best friend to have is a good auntie so I hope you don't mind me adopting that nomenclature for you as you are the best friend I could have.

I have been at Ashgrove for a full month now and am loving it despite that I miss you terribly. The food continues to be good and Michael has been true to his word and made me chicken drumsticks – yummy yummy. I now spend quite a bit of time outside which is very interesting. I don't go too far and am very careful when there are cars about as I reckon they could be a bit dangerous for a little kitty like me. I like playing with Stella even though she can be a bit rough but I get my own back by jumping out at her from under coats and covers and things. I also love playing with golf practice balls which I bat around the house and sometimes rush around with one in my mouth.

I am not tooo happy with Jane calling me an evil kitten – I think I look the picture of good health and liveliness in that photo – I can assure you that I was not up to anything bad or naughty, far less evil. Some people are a little too prone to exaggeration don't you think.

Michael and Jan send you best wishes and I send you all my love

Monny

14/6/2014

My dear Monny,

How beautiful you look in your photo that Michael sent and not at all 'evil'. I'm sure you have not been up to anything bad or naughty as it isn't in your nature. I think perhaps Jane has been influenced by many generations of people who have misunderstood cats and thought them evil.

In fact, the 'Black Plague' started when people began to kill cats and black ones in particular. They thought that black cats belonged to witches and that witches should be burnt at the stake for heresy. But getting rid of so many cats meant that rats survived and the rats carried the bubonic plague that killed so many people. I guess that is cat karma in a way.

I'm so pleased you are getting along with Stella and have learnt to play with her. Just remember that you are smarter than her and keep those claws in if she gets too rough.

I'm also pleased you are practising your golf but don't be too clever and show Michael that you are better at it than he is. Humans can be very sensitive about their golf handicap.

How clever of you to not wander too far from the house while exploring your surrounds and you are very wise to keep away from cars. So many cats think they can outrun a car but sadly that isn't the case.

We are still very busy here and have some new little kittens who were found in a vacant lot, very cold and very hungry. You will be pleased to know someone heard their pitiful cry and handed them to us to look after. I'm now foster mum to them and we love watching them grow into happy little kitties.

We also took a pedigree Tonkinese cat from someone who couldn't look after her and her babies. It seems the owner was only interested in the money the babies would bring to feed her drug habit. So this poor little mum was in very poor condition when she came to us and it was very rewarding seeing her transform from a little skeleton into an exotic looking cat. Her babies have all gone to new homes too.

I'm so pleased Michael has cooked some chicken drumsticks for you as I know it is your favourite. Our poor little Tonkinese mum didn't know what proper food was until she came to us and you should have seen the smile on her face when I took her food bowl to her. It is now her favourite as well and happily she is now with a new owner and being very spoilt.

I don't mind in the least being called your Aunt...I am aunty to many kittens and cats but I still take an interest in every one of you and love to hear how things are going in your new homes.

Which is why I love to hear that you are happy and so settled with Jan and Michael.

Please pass on my best wishes to them and tell Jane that you are very beautiful and not at all evil.

Your loving Aunty Joy. Xx

29/6/2014

Dear Aunty Joy,

I can hardly believe another month has gone by. I have learned a lot about Ashgrove since I last wrote to you. I have discovered the shed which is about 100 metres from the house and it has lots of exciting things in it. I go with Michael when he prepares the horses' feed. I play in the hay and chase rats and mice which is really good fun. I don't go up to the horses yet because the paddocks are a bit too wet but probably will when the weather improves.

I am attaching a photo of me and Jane's daughter Olivia who, would you believe, came all the way from Hollywood just to meet me. She only stayed one night but it was lovely and she gave me lots of cuddles.

Yesterday I climbed a gum tree that had crows in it; Jan thought I couldn't get down again but of course I could but I let Jane help me anyway just to please Jan; there is just so much to entertain me here.

I now have my meals at the same time as Stella – I rush to the

laundry bench where my bowls are, high enough so Stella can't reach them, and Michael fills them before feeding Stella outside. Then when Jan and Michael have a drink in the evening Stella and I have treats with them and then have a little play while Michael gets the dinner.

Thank you for all your news and the beautiful photos of your new babies – of course they are not as pretty as me but then again all kittens can't be black can they.

All my love,

Monny

LETTERS FROM A LITTLE BLACK CAT

13 July 2014

My Dearest Monny,

What a lovely photo of two very beautiful young ladies. You must feel very special having a visitor from Hollywood come especially to see you, but I suspect she also came to see Jan and Michael as well.

You are looking more beautiful (if that is possible) so you must be very well looked after. It must be that fresh country air and all the excitement that goes with accompanying Michael on his rounds of feeding the horses.

All those trees to climb, mice and rats to chase and playing with Stella must make your days very exciting...much more exciting than chasing siblings in the foster home. I'm so pleased you are getting along with Stella as dogs can be fun as well but very wise not to share your food bowl with her. Cats of course have no problem sharing dog food and the grass is always greener in someone else's food bowl.

We are feeling a little sad here as our last hand raised little baby went to his new home yesterday. They were such a delight to have and were such good babies. I've added a photo of one of them because we think he is handsome enough to be a star. He was very cute too and always managed to pose for photographs.

We should have named him Brad Pitt but his new owner called him Basil instead. Basil is not really handsome enough for this gorgeous boy. It seems that from your photo you are having the best life a beautiful little cat could wish for.

Please pass on my very best wishes to Jan, Michael and Jane and make sure you give them extra cuddles and purrs to say thanks.

Your loving Aunty Joy. Xx

31/8/2014

Darling Aunty Joy,

Attached is a photo of me playing with my boot lace on my new scratching post which I love.

Spring arrives tomorrow thank God because we have had nasty frosts here which make my paws very cold in the morning but apart from that I love it at

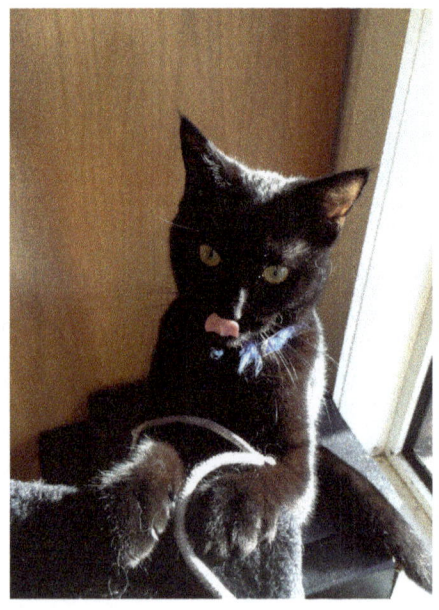

Ashgrove. Do you realise that it will soon be my birthday and Michael has promised me a special treat which is going to be a surprise. I am not sure I can wait till the end of October but I doubt Michael will surprise me earlier even though I have been very good.

All my love,

Monny

1/10/2014

Dearest Monny,

What a darling little girl you have grown into but I'm disappointed you were caught with your tongue out. I do hope you haven't forgotten your manners and it wasn't a reference to what you are being fed or what was said to you. That would never do!

How exciting for you to experience spring on the farm with all those new smells in the air, new flowers and of course new babies. I'm not sure if there are new babies there but it is hard to imagine you were a little baby just a year ago. How time flies.

I'm wondering what special treat Michael has for you for your 1st birthday. Perhaps your favourite chicken drumsticks or perhaps some minced chicken hearts.

I recently returned from a holiday in Italy and saw some cats, some were very well cared for and some were street cats. In Rome there are cats among the ruins, a throwback to the time when Cleopatra gifted some to Julius Caesar, but he set them free as he was allergic to them. Since then, they have been roaming around the ruins, keeping the rats and mice down and hoping some kind strangers would feed them. We saw lots of food bowls around for the street cats but there was also a cat sanctuary with volunteers from around the world who help look after them. They also desex and vaccinate them so are able

to keep the numbers down. It was very heartening to see that people around the world are now starting to care about what happens to cats and make life better for them.

I wish they could all have the happy life that you have and I'm so pleased you love it at Ashgrove. Just make sure you keep appreciating Michael, Jan and Jane with lots of cuddles and purrs. That seems to be all the reward they love the most.

My best reward is to continue to see you happy and enjoying your home.

Please pass on my best wishes to your family and I've added a couple of photos of the Gatti di Roma.

All my love,

Aunty Joy. xx

2/11/2014

Darling Aunty Joy,

Well, I have had my birthday and now am a big girl – one year old who would have believed it? You were right, I did get minced chicken hearts which I gobbled up over the last few days. I also got some toys one of which is a very silly running rodent – I think Michael thinks I am dumb enough not to know the difference between a toy mouse and a real one but he did try so that is something and I love my new ping pong balls. I had an adventure on Friday; Thursday was very hot and Michael left the windows of his car open. On Friday morning I was having a little sleep in it when he drove off to go and check his calves; I had to cry out to tell him I was there and he turned back and brought me home. I wasn't really frightened but he thought I might be and gave me a cuddle before going back to work.

I loved hearing about your trip to Rome and the history of Caesar's cats – how interesting and I am glad they are being cared for.

I still love living at Ashgrove even though it is very different from living with you.

All my love,

Monny

17/11/2014

My dear Monny,

Wishing you a very belated Happy Birthday. What a gorgeous girl you have grown into and what a charmed life you lead.

I'm sure you had some wonderful presents for your birthday along with your new cat scratching tree. Was that the surprise Michael had for you?

I'm so pleased you weren't frightened when Michael drove the car to see the calves but remember to be very careful around cars. How clever of you to alert Michael that you were there and not panic.

We are very busy now with kitten season in full swing. We have made quite a difference here on the Peninsula and the numbers coming through the shelter have dropped significantly. Unfortunately, there are still a lot in other areas which need our love and care. I have two dear little kittens who were found in a box near an industrial estate. Thankfully, some kind person noticed and handed them to us so they now have full tummies and happy faces.

Please pass on my best wishes to Michael, Jan and Jane and I'm ever so pleased to hear how happy you are at Ashgrove.

Once again Happy Birthday to a very special little girl and may you have many more.

All my love

Aunty Joy xxxx

24/12/2014

My dearest Monny,

This will be your 2nd Christmas in your home and what a lovely life you have. It must seem a distant memory all the other kittens you played with, all the vet trips with your ear, and learning about all the new smells and animals in your new home.

Just remember that the glittery baubles are meant to stay on the Christmas tree and are not toys to skittle across the floor. Also, the tinsel needs to stay on the tree and not be used as a means to trip people over with. And finally, even though you are important, remember that the presents under the tree are for your human carers and should be opened by them and not you.

Please send my best season's greetings to Michael, Jan, Jane and all the other members of the family and may you all have a new year full of good health and many blessings.

Happy Christmas, sweet girl.

Love from Aunty Joy xxxx

25 December 2014

Darling Aunty Joy,

Thank you so much for your Christmas Greetings (you beat me to it). I must say I remember very little about my first Christmas because every day with you was like Christmas. You will be happy to learn that I have not climbed the Christmas Tree or attacked the decorations (perhaps if there were a bird or two I might be tempted) but I remember well the manners you taught me.

Jan and Michael have a visiting pup for 10 days and whilst she is quite sweet, she is a bit of a handful and a bit rough to play with.

AND SHE STOLE MY DINNER!!

Jan got me some more food and Michael has poached me some chicken breasts so they have to be careful I get them rather than the pup. She even climbs up onto my food bench so Michael is going to put up a grille to stop her but not me – how good is that?

Stella has asked me to thank you for sending her such a lovely playmate (that's me you see) and I like her too.

Jan, Michael, Stella and the horses wish you a very happy Christmas as do I.

With all my love,

Monny

29/3/2015

Darling Aunty Joy,

I am sorry it has been so long since I wrote to you; life has been rather busy at Ashgrove. First Jan took a trip to Scotland for two weeks at the start of February and I was left with only Stella and Michael – he really isn't too bad you know even though he refused to feed me at 4 am like Jan does – I had to wait until he got up but that was only for 14 days. Of course his knee is not as good as Jan's but I sat on it anyway and purred just to make him comfortable. I even do it sometimes even though Jan is back.

There is a new grey horse at Ashgrove which is very cute. His name is Rosco and I like him a lot – of course from a safe distance but he seems to like me too. Stella is being very nice even though she is only a dog but she can be fun to play with.

Michael tells me Easter is coming up and I might get a fishy treat on Good Friday as Jan and Jane don't eat meat then – I think they are a little disgusted when Michael says he is going to have sausages but Stella agrees with him.

I hope the Easter Bunny comes to you with everything you could wish for.

All my love,

Monny

and greetings from Jan, Jane, Michael and Stella

2/4/2015

My Darling Aunty Joy,

I went up the paddock with Jan and Jane, and Jane took photos. What a brave girl I am. The one with the rug on and showing his bottom is my new best friend Rosco. The others are the old ones.

All at Ashgrove hope the Easter Bunny comes to you and brings you lots of chocolates.

Love,

Monny

LETTERS FROM A LITTLE BLACK CAT

4/4/2015

My Darling Monny,

What a wonderful life you lead and you are now quite the farm cat, or should I say the horse cat. I'm sure Rosco feels very reassured having you looking over his shoulder making sure his horse feed doesn't have any mice tracks. You are very clever the way you walk along the rails, balancing between the stalls and not frightening the horses.

We are very busy here with lots of little kittens and mums who were abandoned with their babies. It is nice they now feel safe and always reward us with lots of purrs and headbutts, much like you used to do.

I'm so pleased you were able to look after Michael while Jan was away in Scotland. I'm sure Jan was very relieved to know you kept up the routine of demanding breakfast at 4.00 am and not so understanding of Michael to insist you wait until he had his breakfast.

May I wish you all a very happy Easter and of course no chocolate for you, Miss Monny.

Stay safe around those horses and keep enjoying your wonderful life.

Love from Aunty Joy xxxx

1/8/2015

Darling Aunty Joy,

JOY HERRING

I'm sorry it has been so long since I wrote to you.

I have told you before how all at Ashgrove are totally horse mad but did you know that today is horse's birthday – what a strange thing that they all have their birthday on the same day; I just can't work that one out. But things get crazier and crazier; they now have a horse inside in the living room. They call it a clothes horse and they put it by the fire to dry the washing – it is really great fun to climb on and sometimes I can even pull things off it onto the floor which is also great fun.

It has been very cold here recently so I mostly sit by the fire and keep lovely and warm when I am not helping feed the real horses up the paddock or helping Michael at the computer as you can see in the attached photo.

I hope everything is well with you as it is with me.

All my love,

Monny

LETTERS FROM A LITTLE BLACK CAT

4/11/2015

Darling Aunty Joy,

We both know that Jan is not a witch (or only sometimes) but I was a bit frightened when she wore a silly witch's hat at Halloween. We had strange looking orange things strung around and one they call a pumpkin with an evil looking face. It is quite scary so I stay well away from it. I brought Jan and Michael a mouse as a present but Stella chased it and it ran under the house. Dogs really don't know when they are not welcome.

I am well and driving Michael mad on the computer.

With all my love, Monny.

5/11/2015

My dear Monny,

I'm glad Jan decided to give you a cuddle rather than send you out trick or treating at Halloween. I'm sure her hat didn't frighten you too much either as I know you are a brave little cat.

I have another beautiful little black mum cat we called Nera which means 'black girl' in Italian. She is only very young, probably about 8 months old and came to me very heavily pregnant. Her gorgeous babies (now 7 weeks old) when they were born two of them didn't have tails which means they probably have some Manx in their background.

We think Nera and her babies are very special and they have been a lot of fun, especially watching them develop their little personalities.

I love the photo of you sitting with Michael at the computer but I know how much you enjoy being with him and making sure the computer is kept warm. Computers don't seem to work when they are cold!

Cats bringing gifts is a sign of great affection and I know you love your family enough to share with them. My own cat brought me a rat that was alive and didn't appreciate my screaming and yelling at her for bringing me such an active present. After storming off in a huff after all her hard work, she no longer brings presents for me to share.

Happy Halloween, dearest Monny, and I hope you didn't share the chocolates or sweets, especially with Stella as they will make you very sick.

Please pass on my very best wishes to Michael, Jan and Jane and thank them for sending me another photo of your delightful life.

Much love

Aunty Joy xx

LETTERS FROM A LITTLE BLACK CAT

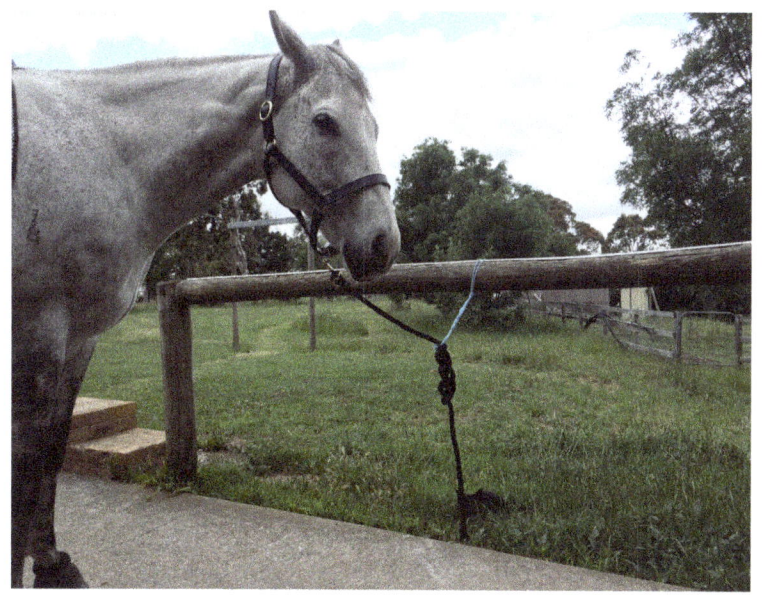

Cat about to pounce on the rope.

1/1/2016

Darling Aunty Joy,

Happy New Year. As you can see from the attached photo taken by Jane I am still having fun at Ashgrove especially with Roscoe.

Michael, Jan and Jane all send greetings.

With all my love,

Monny

JOY HERRING

2/1/2016

Dearest Monny,

A very Happy New Year to you too and especially Michael, Jan and Jane.

I'm so sorry I haven't wished you a Happy Christmas and you beat me to the Happy New Year as well, but I think my excuse is probably a forgivable one.

We have been so busy helping the rural rescues and taking kittens, mums with babies and pregnant cats from country pounds. It is so sad that people take on pets, then don't want the responsibility when it doesn't suit their holiday plans, or worse still, their pretty little kitten has babies of her own.

So, I hope you will forgive my lateness in wishing you all the best in Season's Greetings.

How lovely for you to be able to spend time with Roscoe and the other horses, not to mention running around with Stella. You really do live in paradise so I hope you are very grateful and give everyone lots of cuddles and purrs.

I also hope you didn't overindulge too much over Christmas as I know you like to keep your very svelte figure.

Wishing you all a very Happy 2016 and thank you for the photos over the year. You know how I love to see you happy in your home and my wish for 2016 is that many more of our kittens and mums will be just as happy as you.

Much love to you all,

Aunty Joy

Jane was very interested in adopting a tabby kitten for her family and Michael emailed me about one that they had seen.

3/1/2015

Happy New year Joy and thanks for your lovely email to Monny,

Jane can't help herself hence the email I am forwarding.

I should be obliged if you could reply to me (or Monny).

Warmest regards,

Michael A.

Jane had seen some of our kittens on our Facebook page and showed an interest in adopting one. I had quite a few kittens

available at the time, some with me and the rest with other foster carers. Once again Jane travelled down to see the kittens and was quite taken with a little tabby I had raised.

Jane adopted Ziggy from me and so our story continued with the unwanted intrusion of a young, very pretty, affectionate kitten arriving at the farm for a visit. Monny was not at all impressed.

26/1/2016

Darling Aunty Joy,

Whilst I very much approve of your cat rescue pursuits I am very troubled that you would subject me to the dreadful Ziggy. He has invaded our house, played with Stella and tried to take over everything. Thank God for my darling Jan who protected

and cuddled me throughout this ordeal. I can't understand how you would allow a namby pamby tabby to do this when there was a cat who obviously has the priorities in order.

Please don't get me wrong, I am not being critical but hope you will try to keep Jane in control in the future.

Michael has just come

home from his rotten calves and has given me cuddles and even promises poached chicken (no bones of course) for lunch – whacko!

Much love,

Your ever grateful Monny

29/1/2016

Darling Monny,

Even though you think the world revolves around you I'm afraid there are younger and prettier kittens in this world and it is totally understandable that Jane wants to show everyone her new baby Ziggy.

You may not be impressed but your carers Jan and Michael are very pleased to see Ziggy and I know Jane adores him.

So as a piece of advice, I would welcome this little intruder because he isn't permanent like you are and you can blow raspberries at him as he returns to his own home.

I know you will stomp around showing your great displeasure at Michael and Jan but just remember they feed you so don't push things too far. Just enough to gain a bit of sympathy, then welcome them back into your paws with lots of purrs and headbutts.

You need to be smart in your actions and show great disdain to Ziggy when he comes to visit but don't let the family see it or they may banish you outside and he will get ALL the attention.

If that doesn't work then you will just have to 'suck it up, Princess' because otherwise he will just take advantage of you and edge you out and that would never do.

The best advice I can give you is to be extra smoochy to Jan as she does seem to have a weakness for a sweet little black cat and that is YOU.

Your ever-loving Aunty Joy x

11/5/2016

Darling Aunty Joy,

Do you realise that I have now been at Ashgrove for 2 years and

2 weeks? Gosh how time flies, although I have to admit that it seems such a long time since I left you.

I have found out that the awful Ziggy improves with time and I am now able to tolerate him even though I disapprove how rough he is with Stella and vice versa – they really are beyond the pale leaping and rolling around with each other in a totally undignified manner. I would have thought that Stella would be old enough to behave more sensibly and set some sort of example against thuggery; alas I am wrong.

Winter has started to set in but that doesn't stop me from helping Jan and Jane with the horses which I really enjoy and at least Stella behaves with a modicum of good sense then, but I have to keep a watchful eye on her. Bed is lovely and warm with all the winter bedclothes and I love snuggling up to Jan. During the day Michael lights the fire for me which is really yummily warm and cosy – I share it with Stella.

I really am a lucky girl and have you to thank for such a lovely home.

Jan, Michael, Jane and Stella send their love as would Ziggy if he would just stop a moment to read this.

Big hugs, kisses and purrs from your ever-loving,

Monny

22/5/2016

My dear Monny,

How remiss of me not to reply sooner and I do apologise for taking so long. How wonderful that you have celebrated your amazing life at Ashgrove and your 2 years have flown by. Having a wonderful carefree life on a farm with people who adore you does make time fly and I'm sure each packed day is even more delightful than the previous.

I'm so pleased to hear you are tolerating visits by Ziggy and although he is young, handsome and charming I'm sure you can hold your own by being your darling sweet self.

I'm also sure that Stella is enjoying having two cats to entertain as dogs like to include everyone – whether they want it or not.

I'm also so pleased to hear that you are helping Jan and Jane with the horses and then settle near the fire with Stella for your afternoon snoozes. That is my favourite place as well, although my cat is a bit fatter and sitting on my knee doesn't last very long.

I have been very busy this kitten season and each year I hope things will get easier but alas that doesn't seem to happen.

I have just taken in two dear little tabby kittens who were dumped in the bush to fend for themselves. They of course didn't really know how to catch their own food so when found they were huddled together and very skinny.

I will never understand how people can love and play with kittens, then when they tire of them or it is inconvenient just go and dump them in the bush and forget about them.

Anyway, these little sweeties are now safe with us and once they have been fattened up and had their vet work done, we will try and find them a loving home such as you have.

LETTERS FROM A LITTLE BLACK CAT

Thank you for reminding me of your two-year anniversary and know how much I appreciate how happy you are with Michael, Jan and Jane. I'm so proud of your behaviour towards Ziggy and although you may feel a teensy bit jealous, being the cool cat that you are always wins the day.

Please pass on my very best wishes to Michael, Jan and Jane and a pat for Stella and Ziggy.

Your loving Aunty Joy

30/12/2016

Darling Aunty Joy,

It has been a very eventful year with the arrival of Ziggy. He really is a bit of a handful but I am getting used to him even though he is very boisterous. When he is not here, life is bliss at Ashgrove with Stella, Jan and Michael, all of whom send their love and best wishes for the New Year.

With all my love,

Monny

30/12/2016

Dearest Monny,

I'm sorry I am again late in not wishing you all a very happy Christmas but do wish you a wonderful new year with all your family.

I'm so pleased you have accepted Ziggy visiting even if he is a bit naughty. Boys are a bit like that especially when they want to show off in front of a princess like you. I'm sure you give him your best 'I'm not amused' look and can relax when he goes back home again.

Please wish Michael, Jan, Stella and of course Jane and Ziggy a very Happy New Year and may it be happy and healthy.

Lots of love to you all

Aunty Joy

Our emails became more and more sporadic over time although Jane kept me up to date with the antics of Ziggy and how Monny wasn't very happy when he came to visit at the farm.

Unbeknown to me at the time, Michael was undergoing chemo and radiation treatment for cancer, and although we kept in touch at Christmas, knowing Monny was so happy in her home was the best news I could have had.

It was with great sadness that Jane informed me of the passing of Michael on 22 June 2017.

Michael A Adams was a Queens Council and Chief Magistrate who introduced major reforms including designing and building the children's court, early intervention on drug treatment, an apology to the Aboriginal people on behalf of the Magistrates' Court and championed those with a disability or who were disadvantaged.

Every day Magistrates have to make decisions on cases and sometimes those cases remained with them. Being a Magistrate or Judge can sometimes be a lonely life and most need the companionship of a pet or some outside hobby to take the stresses away.

For Michael he loved animals although it wasn't until he met and married Jan that he learnt to love cats. Michael, like many people grew up thinking cats only killed wildlife, birds in particular. When he married Jan she came with a cat and a dog so it was a case of love me, love my pets. He was also a passionate cook and loved to entertain his guests with his cooking prowess. He also loved gardening and took great pride in the roses that he grew.

Michael always had a black kelpie dog that accompanied

him into chambers. Besides the dog, were his love of horses and new-found love of cats. His dog was black, his horse was black and of course Monny who was black.

I never got to meet Michael in person but through our cat emails I felt I knew him as a compassionate, generous animal lover and of course – we shared a whacky sense of humour.

Monny was a great comfort to Jan in the days after Michael's death and continues to be her loyal companion, accompanying her when she feeds the horses or when she is out in the garden. Her favourite place besides tucking up close to Jan is in front of the fire with her other best friend, Stella. She is even tolerating visits from Ziggy, just so long as he doesn't stay too long.

Acknowledgements

It was while talking to my author friend Elise McCune about her rescue cat Bella that she suggested I write down some of my rescue stories. Having recently retired from running Peninsula Cat Rescue for nine years and having worked on my own before then, I thought about the many cats and kittens I had rescued who could be interesting to write about for this book.

Rescue work often involved us receiving an animal with very few details of their past. Getting them well and healthy for the next part of their journey in their new homes was quite often only a matter of a few weeks' work. So their stories, had I written them, would have been very short.

The twelve stories I have ultimately chosen to tell have had some significance – in bringing cats back to health, turning around a bad situation, and in most cases giving cats new lives in loving homes.

On asking the new owners if I could write about the story of their cats, the answer was always an enthusiastic yes.

I am particularly grateful to Jan Adams and Jane Brook for allowing me to publish the letters from their little black cat Monny, with some help from Michael Adams, and allowing me to name this book in Monny's honour.

Thank you to Carolyn Dornbusch who arrived very early in the morning to take kittens to the nursing home where she worked and brought them home again after her shift finished.

Thank you to Jaimie Andrewartha and her family for allowing me to share the story of Oliver and Oliver's Army of helpers who made it possible.

Thank you to Lake Zamitt, Jeanette Rowe and Marilyn Rowe for the story of Molly.

Thank you to Lauren Brennen and all the staff at PETstock in Somerville for the tolerance and patience you had with Albie. My cats and dog especially thank you.

A special thank you to Faith Moore who spoke out about the horrendous conditions endured by some pedigree breeding cats. Faith didn't hesitate when I asked if I could include Tara in these stories and hopes it raises awareness about these breeding cats.

Thank you also to Leeza Hura from Cats in Action Pty Ltd for bringing Joffrey back to us after his filming debut. He has never forgotten that he was once almost famous.

An enormous thank you to Dr Jim Euclid and the team at Cat Lover's Vet Clinic in Frankston, Victoria. When I started rescuing cats and kittens all those years ago, Jim was the first vet to support my rescue work. His knowledge of cats is extraordinary but he also listened to me when I fought for the life of a cat or kitten. Without Jim, Peninsula Cat Rescue would likely not have existed and his support meant that thousands of cats and kittens went on to live happy lives.

To all the foster carers at Peninsula Cat Rescue Inc. who willingly took cats and kittens into their homes and cared for them. Our rescue, along with many others, would not have been able to save the animals without the volunteers working hard in the background.

To Janine Hanson and Kerry Hawkes from Mallee Cats Rescue in Mildura who worked so hard to bring the cats and kittens up to health before transporting them to us. The odds against you were enormous but you persevered and are now making a difference in your own rural area.

Thank you to Trish Hart for the fabulous book cover. Trish has worked with me right from the beginning of rescue and designed our business cards, banner, logo and wine bottle labels. www.trishhart.com

Lastly, my grateful thanks to Elaine Marriner, Elise McCune, Kate McQuinn, Annemarie Page and Liz Behrendorff for reading these stories and giving an anxious new author feedback, advice and encouragement to keep writing.

About the Author

Joy Herring was President and joint Founder of Peninsula Cat Rescue from 2010 until retiring in August 2019. Her interest in cat rescue began when she assisted her daughter in her voluntary work at the RSPCA in 2005 before moving to the local pound in 2008. It was while volunteering in the pound that she saw the large numbers of kittens, pregnant cats and nursing mother cats that were surrendered or abandoned at the pound. They were often the first to be euthanised because there were so many of them and they were often viewed as competition for the cats looking for a home.

Since incorporation in 2010, Peninsula Cat Rescue has been responsible for rehoming thousands of cats and kittens (all desexed) who would otherwise have ended up as euthanasia statistics.

www.ingramcontent.com/pod-product-compliance
Lightning Source LLC
Chambersburg PA
CBHW062032290426
44109CB00026B/2606